FOR TH

Angela Wheeler

DEDICATION

To my husband Shawn,

and our children Myles, Nelsyn, and Paelyn,

who have given me the family I've always dreamed of.

To our children's Birth Mothers who have

showed nothing less than true love and grit.

To God for choosing us for this amazing journey called adoption.

It's always been your plan, and it's always been your timing. We just

needed to trust and be patient.

ACKNOWLEDGMENT

I've been working on this book since our daughter was just weeks old. After we'd put the children to bed at night, I'd sit at the computer and write for hours on end. I knew in my heart that their stories were extraordinary and that they would like to know them some day. My husband was patient with me as I'd write long into the nights. Sometimes I'd put my writings away for days, months, even years without adding anything to it. Then I'd get inspired or feel nostalgic and pick it up again. Shawn was always supportive of me and my dream of our story one day becoming a book. It wasn't until winter of 2024 when a fire was lit under me that I was inspired to finish this project. Once again, my husband has been nothing short of amazing and supportive. I love you, Shawn. Thank you for everything you do for our family.

TABLE OF CONTENTS

ABOUT THE AUTHOR

Born and raised in Nebraska, Angela Wheeler is a daughter, sister, wife, mother, and friend. Ever since she was a little girl playing with dolls, she dreamt of becoming a mother. Angela works and volunteers at her church. She enjoys spending time with her family, attending her children's activities, and writing in her spare time.

Page Blank Intentionally

CHAPTER 1

As I sat there cradling my newborn baby girl, seated across from me in her hospital bed, my daughter's birth mother told me her story. She had my undivided attention, and indeed, you could have heard a pin drop. No reading, training, counseling, or anything else could have prepared my heart for it. Her story changed me forever. She taught me that life is not fair, but it is worth fighting for.

"For my thoughts are not your thoughts, neither are your ways my ways, declares the Lord." Isaiah 55:8-9

Shawn and I were high school sweethearts at the tender ages of just fourteen and fifteen. We were together throughout high school, only breaking up once. After we both graduated, it was decision time. Either Shawn would join the Navy, or we would get married. We chose to marry in June 1996 when I was almost twenty, and Shawn was just twenty-one.

I was working at a hospital in the mid-'90s. I'll never forget the day I went down to the maternity floor to deliver some mail. I overheard a newborn baby's cry. Right then and there, my entire body was consumed with a strong maternal desire. It was a sudden and striking realization that I was ready to be a mother. That feeling didn't fade until almost twenty years later.

Although we wanted children right away, we agreed to wait a year. During that year, we bought a house and got two dogs. I worked full-time at the hospital, and Shawn had a well-paying job with good benefits at a factory. The first year flew by, and before we knew it, we were ready to start our family. We had it all planned out: three children, each two years apart, and we'd be done by the time we were twenty-five and twenty-six years old. Of course, we thought we'd get pregnant on the first try, so you can imagine our confusion and disappointment when we didn't. That first month turned into twelve months without any success. All we ever knew was people getting pregnant right away. This was bewildering to us. We went to the doctor, and he put me on a medication to treat infertility in women, Clomid. The only side effect of Clomid that we paid attention to was that its use may result in multiple births (such as twins or triplets). We were okay with that, thinking having twins would be fun. In fact, we thought we'd probably have a chance of having multiples anyway because I had twin siblings, and Shawn's paternal grandparents had twins.

Fast forward to three months later - I remember that morning - day one of my first missed period. We had gotten up early to see if I had started my period. I hadn't, and we had already purchased the pregnancy tests. After I urinated on the stick, very shortly after, I saw there were two lines. I ran into the bedroom and started jumping on the bed. I told Shawn I was pregnant! We were so happy! This was late September 1998. We confirmed the pregnancy with a blood test at the clinic the next day. Our families knew of our struggles and were aware we had gone to the doctor to get on meds. But even though our families kept asking, we lied and told them we hadn't had any luck getting pregnant. We wanted to wait to tell them until I was further along. It was hard keeping it a secret because I was both sick and extremely exhausted. At the next doctor's appointment, I had a transvaginal ultrasound where we got to see and hear the heartbeat! On the monitor, it showed the gestational sac with the teeny tiny embryo and its microscopic beating heart. We were amazed at God's handiwork. The doctor checked me and said everything looked and sounded good and told us I was measuring at around 6 weeks. We then got a printout of the ultrasound.

Thanksgiving came, and we were all at our parents' house. That was the day we were going to tell our families I was pregnant. It was so hard keeping a secret that day, but we waited until we were all in the living room following our huge Thanksgiving meal. We had planned to give our parents a gift to announce the news. We wrapped up a yellow newborn outfit and the ultrasound printout and put it in a white sack with blue and pink tissue paper. We gave the gift to them, they opened it, and the next thing I knew, my mom was crying, and my dad was giving me a big hug. Everyone shared our news and congratulated us and gave us hugs. Tears of joy flowed from everyone that day. I never could have imagined this reaction. Everyone was so excited for this first grandchild and was on cloud nine the rest of that night.

We didn't buy anything for the baby until I was further along, mostly because our home was so small we hadn't made room yet. But that didn't stop me from dreaming and making lists of what we'd need and want. Shawn and I even started to think of baby names. Christmas came and went. And then the first part of January would mark three months and the beginning of our second trimester, and we'd have our next doctor's appointment. Shawn and I got to the clinic, and the ultrasound tech said I should be far enough along that she should be able to detect the heartbeat via an abdominal ultrasound and not transvaginally. She got me all prepped and ran the ultrasound device over my belly. We all waited to hear the heartbeat but only heard the squishy ultrasound noise. The tech said it might still be too early in the pregnancy to detect the heartbeat via my abdomen, so she said we'd go back to trying it transvaginally. She left the room, and then in came both the doctor and the ultrasound tech. The tech prepared me for the vaginal ultrasound, and then the doctor inserted the wand. Up on the screen came an image. It was the gestational sac. In the middle of the sac was another image. It was the embryo. We could all see it. There was no movement, no heartbeat. She confirmed what we were all seeing. I started to cry. She did some more work and then told us that according to the measurements of the sac, the embryo had died three weeks ago, meaning I had gone the last month thinking I was pregnant when I wasn't. She said mine was an unusual situation because my body was still producing enough pregnancy hormones that it thought I was still pregnant, and that's why I hadn't started to show signs of miscarriage. Shawn and I were devastated. We both were so unprepared for this news; it was a shock to us. I had had no pain, no bleeding, nor any other indication that something was awry. We left the doctor's office empty-bodied and

3

totally crushed. When we got home, we called our families. Everyone was crying for us. In the midst of all of this, I thought about how our families were so excited for this baby and then thought they'd never be that happy ever again. That was a Friday. The doctor told me that I would need a D&C (Dilation and Curettage) to remove tissue from inside my uterus, and they scheduled it for Monday. I began cramping severely Sunday night and into early Monday morning. Then I started to bleed. My body was finally realizing it wasn't pregnant anymore. The cramps were something awful.

The cramps were excruciating. I had never experienced such pain before. I was doubled over with pain. On Monday, I went to the hospital for the D&C. I woke from the procedure in tears and asked for Shawn. I needed my husband badly to be with me. It was over. Now my body had to heal for a couple of months before we could start trying to get pregnant again.

We used those two months to grieve the loss of our baby. Two months passed, and I got the all-clear from my doctor to start Clomid again and try to get pregnant. We were told that since we had already gotten pregnant before, I would most likely have success in getting pregnant early on since my body's hormones were already activated. We started Clomid, and then we waited. One month, two months, surely three months, I'd be pregnant, but nothing happened. We went back to the doctor. He wasn't concerned because we were still so young; we had "lots of time," he said. We were very discouraged by his reaction. We didn't care how young we were; we wanted this to happen now. But what other choice did we have? Thankfully, he did suggest that we begin tracking my ovulation by using an ovulation test. An ovulation test is a urine test that will indicate when you're ovulating. Ovulation is a phase of the menstrual cycle that involves the release of an egg from one of the ovaries.

Once you are ovulating, then the chances of fertilizing that egg increase. At least now, we had something new to go on to help us succeed in getting pregnant. We bought the ovulation kits at our local drug store and followed the instructions. Like clockwork, I ovulated when I was supposed to, which is around week 2 after your period. My periods were also on time as they always had been; everything was working as it should, so we had no reason to think we couldn't get pregnant. Another three months passed, and then before we knew it had been a year. Our doctor was baffled. The tests he had performed gave him no inclination that something was wrong with me. He finally suggested we see a Natural Family Planning specialist in Omaha.

We went there, and they taught us all about a woman's body and what signs to look for to both get pregnant and abstain from pregnancy naturally without using medications. We learned all about the importance of the mucus my body expelled vaginally. Clear, sparkly mucus meant I was ovulating, and it was time to have sex. Thick, cloudy vaginal mucus meant we could still have sex, but nothing would happen. Here all those years, I thought it was weird that I had vaginal mucus, as no one ever told me it was natural and purposeful for both preventing and achieving a pregnancy! It was all quite interesting what we were learning, and it made a lot of sense. The Natural Family Planning Specialist educated me a lot about my body that day. We quit the Clomid and did the natural family planning thing for six months without any success. By this time, the doctor was finally starting to take us seriously that something might be actually wrong with me.

In the meantime, it seemed as if everyone around us was getting pregnant and having babies: family, friends, neighbors, coworkers, complete strangers. From people who just got married and planned their pregnancies to those who had no intention of getting pregnant at all, yet still were. There were those who had gotten pregnant that first try without realizing what a gift they had received. There were parents who cherished their children and others who abandoned theirs, and fathers who only paid child support. There were those moms-to-be who would complain about their pregnancy and how sick or exhausted they were, whereas I would have given anything to be in their shoes. Then there were those who chose to abort their baby. Right or wrong, I was envious of anyone who was pregnant. It was discouraging and maddening. Why them and not us? I'd stand in front of a mirror with a pillow in my shirt, dreaming I was pregnant. I was desperate to have a giant round belly filled with a growing child. I shopped for maternity clothes in catalogs and envisioned myself wearing them. I wanted so badly to experience the closeness of mother and child during breastfeeding. Child dedications at church were gut-wrenching. So much joy for these families yet so much sorrow for me. I felt so much guilt and told Shawn he should leave me for someone who could have a child for him. (Of course, he said that was a ridiculous notion and that we were in this together for the long haul.) I truly thought no one could ever have wanted or loved a child as much as I would.

The doctor performed some more tests but only found I had some small cysts on my ovaries, nothing big enough or alarming to prevent a pregnancy. He then suggested we have a Hysterosalpingogram done, which checks for blockages in the fallopian tubes that could prevent the sperm from getting to the egg to fertilize it. We checked into the hospital, had the procedure done, and the doctor said everything looked great. He checked me for Polycystic Ovarian Syndrome. There was no sign of that. He did a series of blood tests. I came to find out that I had very high prolactin levels. Prolactin is a hormone that's responsible for lactation and milk production. Higher-than-normal levels of prolactin can cause infertility due to the body thinking it's producing milk (or actually producing milk), among other issues. Too much prolactin reduces the production of the hormone estrogen. It can change or stop ovulation (the release of an egg from the ovary). Women who are breastfeeding (and thus have high levels of prolactin) usually don't become pregnant. We had finally hit a nail on the head! I had a diagnosis: Hyperprolactinemia. The first step was to have an MRI, which confirmed I had a prolactinoma (benign tumor) on my pituitary gland. I'd need to take medication to shrink the tumor and reduce the prolactin levels. I was prescribed a low dose of Bromocriptine.

Treatment would continue until my symptoms lessened (the tumor shrunk) or I got pregnant. I hated taking the medication. The side effects were awful. For the first three hours after taking the medication in the mornings, I'd get so stuffed up in my nose and felt like my brain was being squeezed. It gave me a headache, and it was hard to breathe out of my nose. Then came the hallucinations at night. It was like I was on drugs! I'd wake up in the middle of the night thinking Shawn was someone else and that I was somewhere else. It was terrifying and not a night went by that I didn't wake up at least once having a hallucination. But despite the side effects, the Bromocriptine was working. Blood tests showed low prolactin levels and follow-up MRIs showed no signs of the tumor. We were so encouraged by this despite what I was enduring from the medication. We continued to try to get pregnant using ovulation tests and the Bromocriptine. We did that for about 6 months without any success. It was time to try something different.

I didn't know how much longer I could take having a headache every day and hallucinations every night. That medication really messed me up. Even after ceasing to take it, I'd still have hallucinations. Those would continue on for years to come, even though they did lessen with each passing year. Another six months passed. We went back to the doctor, and he finally said he'd refer us to a fertility specialist in Omaha. We felt like we were getting somewhere, and it gave us renewed hope! We made an appointment with the fertility specialist. The first thing she did was have Shawn provide a sperm sample so she could test his sperm count. He passed with flying colors; his sperm count was exactly what it should have been. At least we could cross that off our list of reasons why I wasn't getting pregnant. Next, the doctor performed a series of blood tests and ultrasounds on me. The doctor presented us with a plan of attack, and we decided to pursue it: Artificial insemination. Artificial insemination, also known as intrauterine insemination, involves the insertion of a thin, flexible catheter through the cervix to inject washed sperm directly into the uterus. (During natural sexual intercourse, many sperm die before they ever reach the uterus.)

But we had our work cut out for us, and this wasn't going to be cheap, and insurance didn't cover it. Once I got my next period, I would have to begin taking injections in my abdomen called FSH (Follicle Stimulating Hormone), which would trigger ovulation. Follicles are underdeveloped sacs in which eggs develop. FSH stimulates the growth of ovarian follicles in the ovary. When an egg matures during a woman's menstrual cycle, the follicle breaks open and releases the egg from the ovary for possible fertilization (the process by which an egg joins with the sperm to form an embryo). A woman is considered to have an adequate or normal ovarian reserve if the follicle count is 6-10. If the count is less than 6, the ovarian reserve could be considered low, whereas a high reserve is greater than 12. Once the home test showed that I was ovulating, I went to my OBGYN in town to perform an ultrasound to check my follicular count (the number of follicles or egg sacs seen during the early part of the menstrual cycle). The meds were working because I had over 10 follicles ready for insemination! But that also meant we had an increased chance of having multiple eggs fertilized. Like I said before, we were okay with having twins, but the thought of triplets or even more was frightening to us. We would never do selective reduction, so we had to be okay with whatever happened. We needed to get to Omaha for the insemination and quickly. We left immediately. Once we arrived at the clinic in Omaha, Shawn had to give another sperm sample.

They washed his sperm, and they prepared me for the insemination. The insemination was quick and painless, and they inserted a small sack in my vagina to keep the sperm from escaping. I was to keep it up there for 4 hours. We were then dismissed to go home. We'd have to wait for two weeks to see if it worked. We were told that we needed to give this at least three months to try for success. This process was like an emotional roller coaster. The highs were great, the lows were awful. And even though I was worn out, I knew I had to persevere. That first try at insemination was a failure. The next month was too. We'd give it one last try. But just like that, we decided we wouldn't.

That's when God placed adoption on our hearts. It's hard to explain how instantaneous it was; the absolute complete being over trying to get pregnant. But I was done. DONE with all it took to get pregnant. The overwhelming need to close that chapter of our lives. Infertility was some of the darkest days of my life. I wouldn't wish it on my worst enemy. It made us strong and definitely put the fight in us. But we were emotionally suffering, and I was hormonally exhausted; we just couldn't do another test, another procedure. All in all, we spent over six years trying to get pregnant. We didn't ever want to hear that word again! Infertility. Nope, we were done. We had always been happy for people who were having babies, yet still, we were envious, but not anymore once we decided to quit trying. We took complete ownership of our decision. We knew that people would continue to get pregnant and that we wouldn't, not anymore, and we were very much relieved. There would be no more tests, no more blood draws, no more medications, no more mucus, no more doctor visits, no more waiting. Waiting for my period to come, waiting to ovulate, waiting to see if I got pregnant. Waiting. Lots of waiting. Then, the letdowns. The awful letdowns. That's all we had done these past six years, wait and be let down. It sure takes a toll on a person, but it definitely taught us patience. I knew I was done trying to conceive once the thought of adoption entered our minds. And God made it crystal clear to us that it was His plan this whole time for us never to have biological children but to have children through adoption. We had never been so sure of anything in our life. We had waved that white flag. We had surrendered. And you know what? We were at complete peace with it. PEACE. We hadn't had that in a long time.

CHAPTER 2

We immediately began the next chapter of our lives: adoption. With adoption, we could finally see the light at the end of the long, dark tunnel we'd been traveling through all these years. It was a faint light, but it was there. That light was the child we had dreamed of having for so long. That light gave us hope. Hope is an amazing feeling, especially since we were without it for so long.

We chose to go through Nebraska Children's Home as we had somehow heard of them at some point. We also knew there weren't any fees for their adoptions, which was an attractive component, especially since we had already spent so much money on trying to get pregnant. We were pretty ignorant, though. They were the only agency we knew of that did adoptions around here. There was always the option to go through an attorney for a private adoption or go with an international adoption, but those options all cost a lot of money.

We went to our first adoption meeting with Nebraska Children's Home. We found out that they had a few restrictions, with one being that we couldn't be trying to get pregnant while going through the adoption process. We had no desire to get pregnant anymore, so it wasn't an issue for us. We learned that even though they didn't have any fees attached to their adoptions (which was unheard of because adoption is very expensive), we quickly found out that there was still a price to pay with all the training, education, and books we had to read. Plus, they highly encouraged us to remember them as our favorite charity in future years. The education, training, and books we had to read to be approved for adoption and stay on the list of potential adoptive families seemed a bit much, and truthfully, it created bitterness inside of us because we had already gone through so much for so long to try to get pregnant, and then here we had to jump through more hoops when any other person could get pregnant, have a family, and have no training at all. We had no choice in the matter. If we wanted a child, this is what we had to do. So yes, even though there wasn't any fee with Nebraska Children's Home, it wasn't free. There was definitely a price to pay.

The other potential adoptive families we met at Nebraska Children's Home were in the same boat as us. All of us desperately wanted a child to become a family. Nebraska Children's Home was honest with us; they said the wait for a child could be months up to years. There was no guarantee, and considering the large pool of potential adoptive families that were also waiting, we had no idea how long it would actually take. Plus, the chance of adopting a second child with them seemed out of the question unless we wanted to wait for many years to adopt again, as they naturally catered to first-time parents.

One thing Nebraska Children's Home promoted and highly encouraged each family to do was be okay with an open adoption. An open adoption meant that you would have some sort of a relationship with the birth mother and/or birth father and/or the entire birth family. An open adoption could be everything from just sending pictures to an actual personal relationship. At first, this was a turn-off. We thought any other parent in this world didn't have to share their children with anyone, and this seemed to be just another thing we had to do to get approved. But once we began hearing stories from real birth mothers and read books about real open adoptions, we realized how vitally important and healthy it could be for both the adoptee and the birth family to have an open adoption. It would break down barriers. It would help the child with identity issues. Upon hearing these stories, we were absolutely convinced that we wanted an open adoption and that it would be the best thing for our child.

In addition to the adoption training, education, and books we had to read, we had to go through the process of getting approved. We had no idea about the amount of paperwork and meetings involved. We understood why we had to do this, but some of it brought up our past infertility journey, and that was painful to relive. And it seemed as if no one could relate to us in that aspect. We had to meet with caseworkers, have doctors' appointments to confirm our health, provide proof of financial security, fingerprints, criminal background checks, etc. We were bound and determined to get on the adoption waiting list as soon as we could, so we wasted no time at all in getting the work done to get approved. It took us about three months total to get everything done.

Once we were approved, Nebraska Children's Home put us on their official waiting list. Next, we had to complete a portfolio of us for potential birth mothers to look at. This consisted of a bound booklet with pictures of us and a "Dear Birth Mother" letter.

Dear Birth Family,

Before you read this letter and get to know Shawn and me through our profile, please know that we cannot begin to understand what you are thinking right now. You have such an important decision to make. You are deciding whether

you will parent your child or place him/her with an adoptive family. Shawn and I hope you are not alone during this decision process and your family and friends are supportive of you. We believe that God has a plan for ALL of us - for you and your unborn child and for Shawn and me. Maybe that plan includes all of us together, but please know that we are very sincere in saying, "May God bless you and guide you in this selection process, comfort you in your times of hurt and uncertainty, and may He be there for you always."

This has been so very, very hard to write. For Shawn and I it acknowledges a loss for us (trying without success to conceive a child), yet at the same time this letter represents a new beginning and hope to come.

Shawn and I have been happily married for 7 years now, but have known each other for almost 13 years. We live in a small, but very "homey" house with our two dogs, Oliver and Hershel. I am a secretary at a hospital and Shawn works for a heating & cooling company. We are Christians and attend the United Methodist Church.

It has been a dream of ours to add children to our family. For almost 6 years we have waited to become parents. Adoption is an answer to our many prayers. With open arms we would welcome your child into our home and Shawn and I would raise him or her to be a good, loving person, to know his or her heritage, and we would educate them so they would respect and understand the decisions that were made on their behalf when they were born. We would love to have an open relationship with you as well.

Shawn and I have learned that it is best for everyone, especially for the child, to know his birth family, if at all possible. This may be just pictures and letters or it may include visits. Like I mentioned before, we would welcome an open relationship.

Being a parent is a responsibility that never ends. We cannot wait to encounter the joys and challenges that being a parent brings!

Shawn and I would love to be the adoptive parents of your child. We want to and will be the best caregivers we possibly can. Thank you for considering us.

God Bless You.

Sincerely,

Shawn and Angela Wheeler

For our cover picture, we chose a photo of us from our fifth wedding anniversary, along with our two dogs. We were thrilled to be officially waiting. We continued to have monthly educational meetings and training with other families who wanted to adopt. We learned about other adoptions that had taken place with their agency, heard testimonies from real-life birth mothers and adoptees, and also testimonies from past adoptive parents. One thing we quickly realized was that there seemed to be no support for us—the couples who were waiting to adopt. No one who could relate to us and what we were going through, nor what we had gone through with our infertility. It was all focused on the birth mother and the adopted child. We were left to our own devices when it came to support for us.

We also met with the counselors and had a home study where they came into our home and made sure it was fit for a child. I specifically remember that during our home study, we were talking and answering questions, and I apparently said something she disagreed with. I was corrected by the counselor after I referred to our future adopted child as a "baby." She said, "You know it's not a baby, it's not going to be a baby forever, it's a child." That really rubbed me the wrong way when she corrected me. Here we just went through six excruciatingly long years of infertility and loss, hoping for a child. We would continue to not have any choice in the matter as to when we were going to be able to have our family, and now people were telling me how to talk about my future child. Anyone else could talk about their future children however they wanted. But apparently not me. I was very hurt and turned off by her comment. I'll never forget that.

A few months into our being approved with Nebraska Children's Home, my cousin Tricia and her husband Mike confided that they were also seeking to adopt as they, too, had trouble conceiving (their second child). Tricia and Mike lived in Omaha and told us of an agency they found there, Adoption Links Worldwide. She said it was nothing like Nebraska Children's Home as they charged for their services. I asked her how much it would cost, and she said it would be approximately $15,000. Woah, that was a lot of money! Yes, we had already had some in savings, but certainly not that much. Come to find out from my cousins that there was a Nebraska Adoption Tax Credit that could potentially cover a large portion of the cost! We were encouraged to hear this. But that wasn't the best part... Tricia said the wait for a child was typically less than six months!

We could hardly believe what we were hearing! Even though Nebraska Children's Home was a great agency, what Adoption Links Worldwide had to offer sounded so much better than waiting from months to possibly years to adopt with NCH. Tricia told us that there was an informational meeting coming up in Omaha, and we should go to it with them. We went to the meeting and met other folks who were

15

also wanting to adopt. There were unmarried women, married folks, people who already had children, and then there were people just like us: married without any children at all. Nancy and Michelle were the counselors there, and Nancy would be our point of contact. We found out that Adoption Links Worldwide contracted with adoption agencies in four different states: Texas, Georgia, Florida, and Mississippi. Adoption Links Worldwide acted as the middleman—they would get us approved (home study, training, counseling, etc.), and they'd take care of getting our profiles sent out to those various states. We also found out that even though we were already approved for adoption through Nebraska Children's Home, we'd have to go through the process of getting approved all over again—all of it: doctors' appointments, paperwork, fingerprinting, background checks, meetings with caseworkers, home studies, etc. Yet we found out after asking them— that there were no additional requirements such as monthly educational meetings or training, reading books, etc., like there were with Nebraska Children's Home. It was like we could go through the work of getting approved and then sit back and relax and wait to be chosen without any strings attached. Just like normal people who were pregnant waiting for their baby to be born. Even though we had learned a lot from Nebraska Children's Home, we loved the thought of not having to jump through constant hoops.

The other thing that they told us at the informational meeting was that they dealt mostly with infant-minority adoptions—meaning a lot of African-American children were placed for adoption. Some adoptive parents want a child who looks like them and are willing to wait. We didn't care. They're all God's children. My husband and I didn't look anything alike, and we weren't blood-related, what did it matter if our children were? Some people want biological or nothing and sometimes that's what they settled for: nothing. Nothing was not an option for us. We didn't care about race; we were desperate, probably too much so. We only wanted our child to be healthy. Honestly, I never really thought about what it'd be like to have a mixed family. We just wanted a family. We'd do anything for a child. My cousins also didn't care what race their child would be.

We left that meeting feeling as high as a kite and were so motivated to get the ball rolling on getting approved as soon as we could. The first thing we had to do was let Nebraska Children's Home know we had decided to go with a different adoption agency. I made that call. They asked why, and I was honest with her. I told her that the wait was shorter and even though they had a fee attached, there were no extra monthly meetings or training we had to go to, less red tape involved. There was nothing she could say to change our minds.

Nancy from Adoption Links Worldwide arranged for us to work with a home study agency closer to our home so we wouldn't have to travel to Omaha for everything, which is two and a half hours away. We were connected to a counselor named Marta in Kearney (I can't remember the name of the agency she was with), which was just a forty-five-minute drive for us. Come to find out, Marta wasn't even married and didn't have any children. We found it odd that someone who had no personal marriage or children experience was giving us training and advice on how to be parents. We thought that was completely ludicrous and it created more bitterness towards adoption. Just another hoop we had to jump through, but we just kept our mouths shut and did whatever we had to do and with whomever we had to do it with to get approved for adoption. (Side note: Even though this is a crazy thought, I think it would be ideal if every single adoption worker had to either have been adopted themselves or had gone through the adoption process themselves. It would make everything so much better for everyone involved to have someone who could truly empathize with them, both adoptive families and birth mothers.)

Going through the adoption process also made us hardened because almost everyone takes it for granted that they can get pregnant at ease; they don't have to have any training, no counseling, no secured finances, no proving their worth to be a parent, etc. The approval process makes you feel like you're guilty of not being capable of being a parent until a complete stranger (adoption counselor, who in our case wasn't even a parent) proves you are. Another sore subject, we found out that people can say the stupidest, most hurtful things, such as "Adoption is the easy way out" or "Once you adopt, you'll get pregnant."

My cousins got approved, and I swear not even a week later they got the call! A baby boy had been born in Mississippi and they were chosen! They named him Joseph and were there in Mississippi and back with him within a week. Joseph was absolutely adorable. We were elated for them but also excited for us that we might get a call very soon too! But we hadn't gotten approved just yet. Not long after, by the end of June, we were officially on the waiting list. When we didn't get a call within a week like our cousins did, we ignorantly began to second guess ourselves if we were even worthy - and it had only been a week! Then, not even three weeks later, we got THE CALL we'd been waiting for. Nancy said a woman named Jocelyn from Texas was due to have a baby girl on August 10, and she had chosen us! Praise the Lord, we were finally going to have a baby! We had long ago chosen the name Carys for a girl, so we named her Carys Joselyn, Joselyn after her birth mother. We bought all sorts of pink newborn outfits, pacifiers, socks, and receiving blankets. We purchased diapers, wipes, bottles, and formula. We packed Carys' bags, we packed our bags. It was like she was already ours. We loved her already!

We didn't hear anything from Nancy until we called her back on Carys' due date. It had been so hard to wait these past couple of weeks without hearing anything at all! Nancy said she also hadn't heard anything yet from the adoption agency in Texas, but she'd let us know when she did. I know she had other clients that she was working with at that time, but we felt like Nancy wasn't working with us at all - like she had forgotten about us. The communication seemed to definitely be one-sided. A week passed. We called Nancy again, and she said she'd call and find out what was going on. We were so frustrated; all we wanted was more frequent updates! We so badly just wanted to contact the agency in Texas ourselves! Why couldn't we just do that? There had been no information or updates at all. It felt like no one cared or could possibly understand what we were going through. It seemed like we were left in the dark. Too bad there wasn't a "What to Expect When Waiting to Adopt" book out there. Something we could read - someone who could at least relate to us. Nancy called us back and said that the adoption agency in Texas hadn't seen or heard from Jocelyn since she had initially chosen us to be the parents. Nancy told us to keep waiting, and yet again, we were left to our own devices, as there was no acknowledgment of our feelings. A few more days passed before we got a call again from Nancy. She told us that they never heard back from Jocelyn and that she obviously had changed her mind and we should get back on the waiting list. We ignorantly thought the reason we hadn't heard anything was she was just two weeks late in having her baby. We wouldn't let it cross our minds that she had changed hers. That's how desperate our thoughts had become. We were completely devastated. I went into a depression almost immediately. It was the last weekend in August and the State Fair was in Lincoln, so we decided to get away and get a hotel for a couple of nights there and spend some time at the fair. Being away in Lincoln did help, but once we got home to reality, the depression came back, although not as bad as it was before. We were grieving over the loss of a child that was never ours to begin with. But it helped to know that we were back on the waiting list again. We put away our suitcases and put the baby stuff in storage. We didn't want to and just couldn't bear to look at it. It was a reminder of yet another loss in our life. We went about our lives, and the grief lessened a little more each day.

About the second week in September, we got another call from Nancy. We had been chosen again! This time by a woman named Ariana who lived near Atlanta, Georgia. She was due to have a boy and had chosen us to be the parents of her unborn son who was set to arrive any day! Again, we were so excited, but this time, we proceeded with a more cautious approach. "Cautious Optimism" is the term used in the adoption world. But surely, this one would work out for us! "God, please have mercy on us and let this adoption go through!" we prayed. An Open Door was the name of the adoption agency in Georgia and was based out of Thomasville. We told our families, friends, and co-workers, and then we waited to hear ANYthing at all from Nancy. We sure didn't have to wait long. Within a couple of days, we found out that Ariana wanted to have a conference call with us! We set it up for an evening that would work for everyone. That night we nervously dialed Ariana's number. Ariana answered, and immediately I could detect an accent. On the call, she referred to me as "ma'am" and Shawn as "sir."

That was the first time I'd ever been called "ma'am." But that was part of her southern charm. Ariana asked questions about us. We asked her questions about her. She asked us if we had figured out a name yet for the baby, and we told her we chose the name Myles Ahren; Ahren after her first name, Ariana. "Myles!?!" she said? She sure didn't sound too impressed by that name, but what I wanted to tell her, even though I didn't, was, "Listen, lady, we'll name him whatever you want us to!" We seriously thought we had just given her a reason to change her mind about us because of the name we chose. That call was amazing; we talked for a good thirty minutes. It was the first time we had communication, and we needed it to continue in order to have hope about this adoption happening. That conference call was on a Thursday.

Even though things were looking promising, we didn't buy anything more than what we already had, and we didn't pack any bags. We were still very skeptical, especially since the last adoption fell through the way it did. We were definitely more cautious this time. We waited. The weekend came and went. Monday we heard nothing. We called Nancy, and she said she hadn't heard anything either. We waited some more. That was such a long week without any communication from the adoption agency! Naturally, since we hadn't heard anything, we began to doubt that this adoption would go through as well. Then a call came in to me while I was at work on Friday afternoon at 2:00 pm. It was Nancy with Adoption Links Worldwide. She had called to tell us that Ariana had had the baby that morning in Atlanta! She was following through with the adoption and still wanted us to be the parents! Nancy told me that we'd need to plan on being in Atlanta for up to twelve days. She explained to us that in Georgia, the law states that a birth mother cannot relinquish her parental rights until twelve days have passed. And also that if she claims to not know who the birth father is (therefore he wouldn't be able to come forward and relinquish his parental rights) they'd have to run an ad in the local paper daily for forty-five days announcing the 'birth of a baby boy born in Fulton county in Georgia' to see if anyone comes forward to claim the child. We understood the risks, but yet we really had no idea what we had just gotten ourselves into and what the next two weeks would be like.

20

We left our workplaces and called our families to let them know what was happening. Shawn looked into flights and got one to Atlanta for the next evening (Saturday) out of Omaha. We had less than twenty-four hours to get our bags packed and find someone to watch our dogs, and get the house ready for a baby. It was an exciting time for sure! We barely got any sleep on Friday night as we were beyond excited. Saturday afternoon we left our home for the Omaha airport. We arrived in Omaha, boarded our flight, and then we were off! We arrived in Atlanta at 1:00 am Sunday morning. The first thing we noticed was how hot and humid it was there compared to back home in Nebraska. And that was even in the middle of the night! We got our rental car and then began the drive to our hotel. It seemed like we were driving in circles, but we eventually made it. (Shawn had gotten a packaged deal when he booked our flight, hotel, and rental car for less than $2,000. It was an excellent bargain!) We arrived at our hotel at 2:30 in the middle of the night and settled in our room. It was a gorgeous hotel. We would be up again soon to head to the hospital to meet the caseworker, her name was Charlotte, to take us to see Ariana and the baby. We woke up Sunday at 6:00 am and were in the car by 6:45.

Even though the hospital was only thirty minutes away, we wanted to find it early, so in case we got lost, we'd still have plenty of time. We easily found Grady Memorial Hospital and figured out where we'd park and enter. Then we left and went out for breakfast since we still had a little less than three hours before we'd need to be back at the hospital to meet Charlotte, Ariana, and the baby. Breakfast was at a small 'hole-in-the-wall' cafe. I had grits for the first time ever. They weren't too bad! We couldn't help ourselves; we told everyone at the cafe that we were going to meet our new baby.

After breakfast, we ventured back to the hospital. We were still early, but decided to go inside anyway. We went to the gift shop and the cafeteria and then back to the gift shop. We were chomping at the bit to meet Ariana and the baby. We were in the lobby when a very nice woman asked us if we were The Wheelers. We said we were, and she shook our hands then gave us each a hug and told us her name was Charlotte and that she was the case worker assigned to this adoption.

She had been meeting with Ariana the past couple of weeks. Charlotte was so extremely nice! She asked us if we were nervous, and we said yes, but it was a good kind of nervousness. She led us to the elevator, and we went up. We followed Charlotte down a series of corridors in the maternity ward and then we were there.

She knocked on the door, and we entered. At first sight was a woman who was clearly not Ariana. We realized this was an adjoined room. We greeted the woman. Only a curtain was separating us from Ariana. Charlotte softly announced to Ariana that she was here with The Wheelers and asked if now was a good time to visit. Ariana said "yes," and Charlotte drew the curtains back. There she was sitting on her bed...Ariana, the woman who so bravely had chosen to make an adoption plan for her child. She was a little younger than us; I believe she was 24 years old. She was very pretty, dressed in a blue denim dress, and her hair was in braids, and she had the longest fingernails I think I'd ever seen in my life. (How on earth she was able to ever take care of a baby with those nails on I'll never know!) And she was holding a tiny baby boy wrapped in a blanket. He had sleek black hair and at first glance truly looked Caucasian to us and not African-American at all. (We were expecting to find a baby with darker skin - Baby Joseph, who my cousins adopted, had darker skin when he was born so we were expecting the same with this baby.) But we didn't care what he looked like. It was truly love at first sight. We introduced ourselves and gave her a hug. We asked her how she was feeling, and she asked us how our flight had gone. There was some small talk before she'd finally asked us if we wanted to hold the baby.

Of course, we did. It was the moment we had waited for the last six-plus years. I carefully took the baby from her and cradled him in my arms. I couldn't believe this was happening. Shawn and I looked lovingly at him as if he were the most precious thing we had ever seen in our lives. And he was. He started to whimper a little, and Ariana said he was probably getting hungry. She handed me a bottle and asked if I wanted to feed him? She then told us that she had nursed him up till now and that this was his first bottle. (I secretly panicked thinking she was surely going to change her mind after having bonded with him like that during breastfeeding!) I fed the baby his bottle and burped him. It was time to change his diaper. I was so nervous, I was acting like I had never before changed a diaper before in my life, but Ariana guided me through it. Then we swaddled him back up, and he fell asleep in my arms. All of us continued to talk when Ariana's grandmother came in. She introduced herself as "Great Mama Louise" and gave us a hug. She was a beautiful woman. She was there to support Ariana as Ariana's own mother was out on a college visit with her sister, Avonte. We all visited, and then Great Mama just out of the blue asked us what we were going to do with the baby if we changed our minds about him. If WE changed our minds? What was she talking about? We told her we had waited so long for a child and assured her we would never change our minds about keeping him. Never ever.

Ariana was going to be dismissed that day, but the baby had to stay until the next day, Monday. Before long, it was time for everyone to leave. The nurse came with an empty bassinet and placed the baby in it and took him back to the nursery. Another nurse showed up with a wheelchair. Ariana got in it, grabbed her bags, and was wheeled down to the elevator to the hospital's entrance. We all said our goodbyes but promised to meet back at the hospital the next morning for the baby to be dismissed. We drove back to the hotel. It had been a wonderful, blessed day and we were so happy, albeit exhausted. We had to change hotel rooms that night for some reason I can't remember. But then we settled into the room we'd call home for the next twelve days and nights. We unpacked the suitcases and went to the nearest pharmacy to buy newborn-sized diapers after we realized the diapers we had packed were way too big for the baby. We loaded up the car seat and packed the baby bag in the car. That felt unreal to us to be doing that. We had dreamed of this moment for so long!

It was late by the time we got everything ready, and then it was time for bed. It would be the last ever night of just the two of us. God willing, tomorrow we'd be bringing home our baby and becoming a family. Even though we were so completely exhausted, we could barely sleep that night and the morning couldn't get here soon enough. We woke early Monday, got dressed, ate breakfast, and were ready to head out by 8:00 am.

We met Charlotte, Ariana, and Great Mama Louise at the hospital at nine. (We still couldn't believe she hadn't changed her mind about the adoption!) Charlotte led all of us up to the nursery where the baby was. There he was behind a glass wall in his bassinet. Charlotte entered the nursery to be with the baby. We watched as she dressed him in his going-home clothes, a yellow open-ended gown that we had gotten him. It was then time for him to be discharged from the hospital. Charlotte held him in her arms as she was wheeled outside in a wheelchair. Once we were all outside, we were free to take him with us. Shawn left to get the car, and I was there alone outside the hospital with Ariana, Charlotte, Great Mama ~~Louise~~, and the baby. Charlotte handed me the baby, and I didn't know what to do. So I handed him ~~back~~ to Ariana. Charlotte gave me this stern look like, are you crazy woman, what in the world are you doing!? I didn't know what I was doing; I must have panicked or something! I didn't know what to do. It felt weird to be holding him in front of Ariana so I gave him to her. Very soon after I had handed the baby to Ariana, Charlotte said it was time to go and scooped the baby up from her and gently placed him back in my arms. We all said our goodbyes, knowing that we'd see each other again in about a week.

Watching Ariana leave empty-handed was totally gut-wrenching. I couldn't imagine what she was feeling, although I tried my hardest to. I felt so bad for her even though I knew this was a decision she was making. She had made this adoption plan for her child. But here she had just given me one of the greatest loves of her life. After they walked away to go home, I was there all alone, holding this baby. Everything seemed to be in slow motion. Shawn couldn't get to us with the car soon enough. When he did, we loaded the baby into the car seat, and I sat in the backseat with him all the way back to the hotel. I cried the entire way. I was so happy yet so much concerned with what Ariana was feeling.

I felt guilty having her baby, yet this was the moment I had waited so long for. It was all incredibly overwhelming, and I wasn't prepared for these feelings. The first thing we did when we got him settled in his

24

car seat was give him a pacifier. We didn't know if he'd take it or not since he hadn't ever had one, but he took it just fine. We got to the hotel and brought him up to the room. Shawn really hadn't had the chance to hold him yet, so he took him out of his car seat and held him first. I got his bottle ready, and we fed him together. We changed his diaper together. We counted his ten little fingers and his ten little toes together. We were falling in love with him. Shawn said, "Mommy, why don't you take Myles." That was the first time we called him by his name, Myles. And that was the first time someone called me Mommy. I was scared to fall in love with Myles as we still had twelve long days before Ariana could change her mind, but I couldn't help myself. I loved him the moment I laid my eyes on him.

That whole week all we did was love on Myles. We did lots of skin-on-skin contact where he would be naked with only a diaper on and lay on our bare chests so he could hear our heartbeat and feel the warmth of our skin against his. There were lots of rubdowns with lotion. We had learned these were good ways to bond with a child, especially an adopted one. Those were precious moments. We took so many pictures! Back in the day, you couldn't just text a picture from your phone. Phones were for calling people, and that's about it. So we had to fax the pictures to our families and friends. That was the only way to get pictures to them unless we mailed them.

It threw us for a huge loop, getting up in the middle of the night several times, as newborn babies do. We also took lots of naps. We had called down to the front desk quite a few times asking for a crib, yet they never brought one up, so we put Myles in one of the dresser drawers. It was perfect and safe for him, nice and snug, with little room to move. So that's where he slept for twelve nights. We had no schedule, so we slept in late and stayed up late. We frequented The Cheesecake Factory many nights, not even getting there until 8 pm and having coffee and cheesecake at 10 pm. (We determined the vanilla bean was the best kind they had!) We were living the good life with our new baby. But always in the back of our minds was the thought that Ariana was free to change her mind at any time. Each time the phone rang, a chill would run up our spines and a pit would drop in our stomachs as we were convinced it was Charlotte calling to say that Ariana wanted him back. I was on my knees more than once pleading with God to keep this precious baby.

Charlotte was so patient and understanding of our feelings and emotions. We point-blank told her we were afraid we were going to lose Myles, and she reassured us each time we asked her that everything looked to be on the up and up with Ariana. She was constantly reassuring us that Ariana was doing well. It was so nice to know that she was still in touch with her and caring for her. Charlotte had a big job being both Ariana's advocate as well as our counselor. I'm sure she more than once thought we were delirious and high maintenance, yet not one time did she not answer our phone calls or show us kindness and compassion. She was our angel in disguise while we were in Atlanta, and I hope she was Ariana's, too.

Seven days had passed, and we were slowly but surely winding down our required stay in Atlanta. As time drew to a close, even though she gave us no indication at all that she was going to change her mind, we were beginning to doubt more and more that Ariana would actually go through this. We hated to be so negative, but this was all way too good to be true. We were so afraid to lose Myles. We loved him so much, but we knew Ariana did too. We did meet with Charlotte, and Ariana and her entire family again before we left. They met us at our hotel. This time Nana, Ariana's mom, joined us as well as Ariana's sister, Avonte, and also Great Mama Louise, too. We passed Myles around, everyone took turns holding him, but what we really wanted to do was grab him and run in the opposite direction and not look back until we were safe back in Nebraska. Of course, we didn't, we couldn't. Surely Ariana would change her mind after holding him again. I'm telling you we were convinced we weren't going to be able to keep him!

Day twelve of our adoption adventure finally came, marking the last hours that Ariana was able to change her mind/relinquish her parental rights. Our flight was set to leave in the afternoon, just hours shy of the completion of the twelve days. We boarded the flight and off we went. Our plane was delayed in midair over Kansas City because of it being secured airspace for the President. I was getting motion sickness as we had been flying in circles for forty-five minutes straight, plus I was so anxious to get home with my new baby and introduce him to our families. We missed our families terribly. We were still in the disbelief stage that we were actually going to be able to keep Myles and call him our own.

We finally landed in Omaha. We got off the plane and walked down the aisles to find our luggage. Shawn grabbed the luggage, and I was holding Myles. Then we walked to the area where we could exit the airport. There they were. Our families were waiting for us with a homemade poster that said, "Welcome Home Baby Myles." Even my cousins were there with their children to welcome us home. This was an unreal moment, and my knees were shaking uncontrollably and about to buckle, like they were like wet noodles. Everyone was crying. I was never so happy to see my parents as I was when we got back from being gone for those twelve long days by ourselves. I handed Myles to my parents. They cradled him. They were so proud to finally have a grandchild! And my sisters loved their new nephew. It was a joyous moment. On the way home, Shawn drove our car that we had left at the airport, and I rode with my parents, me and my mom sitting in the backseat with Myles in his car seat between us. We finally arrived at our home. Man was it good to be home! We brought Myles into his new house. We had a house full that evening. Lots of family came over to see Myles. Later that night, the phone rang. It was Nana. There it was again, that sinking feeling that she was going to tell us that Ariana had changed her mind. No, that wasn't it at all. She was calling to see if "y'all made it home safe," and "kiss my grandson for me."

I took off three months of work to stay home with Myles. It was the best time of my life, and I enjoyed every moment of it. We sent monthly pictures and letters directly to Ariana, as we agreed we would do for the first year of his life. And we kept in touch with Nana by phone and email every couple of months.

When Myles was six months old, we could finally begin the process of finalizing his adoption in Nebraska. We called the adoption agency in Georgia for them to send the papers to us to begin finalization, only to find out that they had failed to run the forty-five-day birth father ad in the newspaper, and they still had to do that in order to proceed with finalization. So that meant Myles' birth father could still come forward and claim him, even though he had already been with us for six months! We were crushed and very scared once again. Those terrible feelings of doubt came creeping back. The ad ran for forty-five days, and nothing happened. Thank God his birth father didn't come forward to claim Myles. We were able to finally finalize his adoption at the courthouse in Grand Island when he was 11 months old. It was finally official! Myles was going to be ours forever, and no one could ever take him from us!

CHAPTER 3

The plan was always to adopt two children, so it was no surprise when a few years had passed after Myles was born that we were ready to begin the process of adopting again. It was November of 2006.

The journey started by deciding which agency we would adopt through. Would we go with Adoption Links Worldwide in Omaha and potentially Georgia again as we did with Myles, or would we go an alternative route? The gains of going with the same agency were that they already knew us, and we could bypass some of the formalities. However, the huge downside was that in Georgia, the birth mothers get those twelve (excruciatingly long) days to decide if they want to relinquish their rights to their child or, on the contrary, change their mind and decide to parent the child. For us, this arduous twelve-day window of time was a mentally draining disadvantage and outweighed any benefits at all. Therefore, we decided to go a different direction.

Our cousins had adopted their son Joseph around the same time as we did Myles, except that Joseph was born in Mississippi, not Georgia. In Mississippi, the birth mother can relinquish rights after just seventy-two hours (three days)! This seemed to be a more manageable timeframe for us so we didn't have to live in limbo for so long not knowing if we would actually be adopting the child or not. Those twelve days we spent in Georgia not knowing if we would be able to keep Myles or not nearly killed us. Plus, we really didn't have the communication we desired with the agency in Omaha, so we decided to cut out the middleman, Adoption Links Worldwide, and go directly with the agency in Mississippi.

New Beginnings was the name of the adoption agency my cousins went through. They had a wonderful, positive experience with them when they adopted their son, and we could hardly wait to go through them too. We contacted New Beginnings, and before long, the thick packet of paperwork had arrived in our mailbox. Prior to tackling any of that business, the first step was getting a Home Study completed. Since we obviously couldn't have someone in Mississippi do one for us, we were advised to contact different adoption agencies in Nebraska to find out if one of them would be willing to complete (just) the Home Study for us. We chose Lutheran Family Services. Roberta would become our case worker, and she was an angel from the beginning. She was the sweetest person, and we were very, very thankful to have her along for the ride. We filled out mounds of papers and forms and also met with Roberta a handful of times. Then she came to our home to not only meet Myles and observe us being a family, but also to make sure our home was indeed suitable for another child. We had spent hours cleaning and making sure everything was perfectly in its place, but when Roberta arrived, it was quite obvious she could care less about the state of our house; she was only interested in our family dynamics. She made us feel very comfortable, and we actually enjoyed having her in our home. Soon, our Home Study was approved.

Next, we would begin the mountain of paperwork and procedures necessary to be approved for adoption in Mississippi. This would include fingerprinting, criminal background checks, financial explorations, reference inquiries, physical examinations, etc. Not to mention the plethora of questions we had to answer and items that needed to be mailed in. To be approved for adoption is not for the faint of heart. It is very time-consuming and quite tedious. I always felt that every single person should have to fill out paperwork and go through all of this before they were allowed to ever have a child, but that's obviously not the way God intended it. If that was the case, there would be a lot of people who would decide not to have children and/or people who would be found not fit to have children.

It took a good solid two months to get approved and finally be on the adoption waiting list. The absolute last thing we needed to do was to put together a portfolio that included pictures and information about our family, as well as a 'Dear Birth Mother' letter. The portfolio was something we took very seriously and we wanted to make sure we were well-represented so that there would be no doubt in a birth mother's mind once she saw our pictures and read about us.

Dear Birth Mother,

We are so grateful you have chosen life for your baby! You're reading this letter because you are considering making a life plan for your child. We admire your courage so much. Thank you for taking a moment to learn about us.

Three years ago, our prayers were answered. It was through the beautiful gift of adoption that Shawn, Myles, and I became a forever family! Our hopes are to once again welcome a son or daughter into our family. It is so exciting to imagine another child in our lives!

Shawn and I embrace what being a father and mother means to our son. And we will love and nurture this child with all of our hearts and beings as well. We will love this child as completely as if he/she were born to us. Our families will never, ever forget the gift of love that was given.

We can't begin to express our deep gratitude, nor can we imagine what you are going through at this time. You are admired so much. We are praying for you and we ask God to comfort, guide, and give you strength.

Shawn and I hope you might consider our family in this extremely important decision you are making. It's because of this selfless gift of love, through adoption, that we can even dream of becoming parents again.

God Bless You.

Most Sincerely,

Shawn and Angela

Now that that was completed, we could begin the fun part: planning for the baby to come home! The thing with adoption is you never know when it's going to happen; my cousins adopted their baby a mere one week after being approved, and Myles' adoption only took three months after we were approved. So right away, I went to Walmart and excitedly purchased all the essentials: newborn diapers, ointment, pacifiers, bottles, formula, burp cloths, receiving blankets, a couple of gender-neutral outfits, onesies, baby wash, lotion, etc.; any item needed to take care of a newborn. I was on cloud nine while shopping, and anyone who saw me and my cart full of stuff would have thought I was actually expecting a baby. Well, I, in fact, was! Just not in the traditional way. I brought the stuff home, washed up what I could, then packed all of it in the baby's suitcase and stored it away in the closet so all we had to do was grab it and go. I thought about also packing a suitcase for Myles, but since we didn't know when this was going to happen and what type of weather we would be having, that would probably have been a waste of time. So I decided to just wait on packing Myles' suitcase until the time came. What I did do, though, was make a list of stuff he'd need so we wouldn't miss a thing, and all we'd have to do is go down through the list and pack what was on it.

We were approved in October 2006. Again, we had no idea how long we'd be waiting; it could be one week up to a year or longer. Well, a couple of months had passed, and we had heard nothing from the adoption agency. Then one February evening, a Friday, we had been out to supper, and when we got home, I checked the phone and saw we had a missed call. I looked at the caller ID and it showed it was a Mississippi number! Oh my gosh, only one reason why a Mississippi number would be calling - a baby! I saw that there was a flashing red light on the phone, meaning there was a message. I checked the message and then literally screamed! We received the call we had been longing for: "This is Debbie with New Beginnings. could you please call us back at your earliest convenience?" I called her back as quickly as my fingers could dial the number. Debbie answered and gave us the message we had been waiting for a Birth Mother is due to have a baby boy, and she has chosen us to be the family! We just couldn't believe it. One minute, we're eating supper, and the next, we're planning for a baby! Debbie told me she'd be in touch with us as soon as the birth mother went into labor but that she was due at any time now. I asked her what the birth mother's name was so we could pray for her and also fashion a middle name for the baby from her first name. Her name was Teresa. As soon as we got off the phone with her, we called all of our family to let them know we were going to be having a new baby boy real soon!

We rushed to get Myles' suitcase packed as well as ours. Let's see, weather in Mississippi in February? We looked it up on the internet, and it sounded like it was pretty decent so we packed long-sleeve shirts and pants, but no winter coats or gloves, etc., because it didn't seem like we'd be needing anything more than a jacket. I told Shawn he needed a haircut, and he got one the next day. He also cut Myles' hair. We got quotes from the rental car company and had a van more or less on hold for when we would need it. We were all ready to leave. The only thing we didn't have planned was who was going to take care of the dogs. But that was something we knew our family could help us with if we were in a pinch. We went about our normal lives knowing that at any time, we would be getting a call. Do you know how hard it is to concentrate on anything when you know your baby is going to be born at any given moment? That week dragged on and on and on with no call from the adoption agency. We began to wonder if she had changed her mind. Then the call came in: she was in labor and heading to the hospital, and we should plan on leaving at any time! That was a Sunday. That weekend, Myles had started to get sick and by now had a cough and a high fever. With it being a Sunday and a baby on the way, the only thing we could think to do was take him to the ER. We got to the ER, and the doctors tested Myles for Influenza, pneumonia, and Respiratory Syncytial Virus (RSV). The test for RSV came back positive. They sent us home with a nebulizer and medications. We started those treatments right away and of course hoped that Myles would be feeling better very soon because RSV was so highly contagious, especially for newborns, and that was the last thing we wanted to do was have a sick baby.

The next morning could not get here soon enough. The first thing we both did was call into our jobs to let them know we would be leaving for our baby. Next, we called the car rental place and finalized the rental of the van, and Shawn went and picked it up. We packed all of our stuff in it. Then we boarded the dogs at the vet. Now all we had to do was wait for the call, climb into the van, and we'd be out of here. Monday could not have gone any slower, and every time the phone rang, we practically jumped out of our skin, thinking it was the adoption agency. It wasn't. We passed the time in the evening trying to figure out a name for the baby and then how it would be spelled. I hadn't quite convinced Shawn yet to name the baby Nelsyn, and Isaiah was next on the list so we both agreed on the name Isaiah Trace, Trace after the birth mother's first name, Teresa.

Monday came and went. No call. Tuesday came and went. Again, no call. Our hearts sank, and we had a strong gut feeling it wasn't going to happen at all. We finally got in touch with Debbie, and she said the adoption was still on but that the baby hadn't been born yet. Wednesday came and went. No call. Finally, on Thursday, we made some painful decisions. We called Debbie. We had changed *our* minds; we just couldn't keep going on like this. We unpacked the van and took it back to the rental company. There was no reason to keep paying for it if we weren't going to use it. We also picked the dogs back up from the vet. Friday, we went back to work, and Myles went back to daycare. Debbie from the adoption agency called late Friday morning and said that the birth mother was back in the hospital and in labor and she still wanted us to be the parents.

Even though we desperately wanted to say yes, we had already made the excruciatingly tough decision that we would not be adopting Teresa's child. In our minds, if she had been that wishy-washy and not in touch with us the first time she was supposedly in labor, then what would our future be like with her? Would she change her mind and want to parent her child? She seemed too high of a risk, so we told Debbie "no." She was shocked, of course, and I guess she sort of understood where we were coming from, but there's absolutely no way she could have fully understood unless she herself had gone through what we just had. (Come to find out, Teresa did indeed eventually have her baby, and she did make an adoption plan for him.) Even though our hearts were broken, and we were very frustrated because of the finances we had already spent, we had no regrets at all saying no to it because of what we had already endured. There would be no baby for us, not this time, at least. Isaiah Trace was not meant to be ours.

That was February. The coming months seemed to drag on and on. After a couple of months had passed, we became afraid that the adoption agency was somehow punishing us for not adopting Teresa's baby boy and thus withholding any potential adoptions from us. Of course, this was absolutely not true at all, but when you're waiting for a baby that could come at any moment, your mind begins to wander in directions it has no business going in. Now I know the reason why we weren't chosen yet by any birth mothers - it was because our baby, the one that God had long ago chosen for us, hadn't been born yet.

We got in touch with Debbie from New Beginnings to make sure everything was still on the up and up and that our portfolio was still out there for potential birth mothers to view. She reassured us that all was good and that sometimes being chosen can take months, whereas some only take a few weeks. We asked her if we needed to make any changes to our portfolio, and she said it was fine as it was. We basically just needed to be patient. That was May. We continued on with our lives as usual, with the notion in the very back of our minds that we could be chosen any day.

July 31 was a Tuesday. I was at work that afternoon when I received a call from Debbie at New Beginnings. I took the call in an empty office so I could have privacy. Debbie told me the absolute best news: if we wanted him, she had a one-week-old baby boy waiting for his forever family to come pick him up! Even better was that the seventy-two hours/three-day wait before the birth mother could sign relinquishments had already passed, so he was ours for keeps! All we had to do was pick him up from his foster home and wait a couple of days to finalize at the courthouse in Mississippi! (The fact that we wouldn't have to wait for relinquishment was such great news after all the stress and turmoil with Myles' adoption and, of course, what we had just experienced months before with Teresa's baby.)

Debbie gave me all the details, and I wrote them down as best as I could so I could relay them to Shawn. She said he had been born on July 25 (almost exactly 9 months after we were approved!) and that his birth mother's name was Kadenya. She wanted a closed adoption. He was healthy, and there was no history of substance abuse with his birth mother while she was pregnant with him. He was staying at a Foster Home, and Gary and Diane Adkins were the names of the foster parents. (Debbie said they were the absolute sweetest people ever and were taking very good care of him. She gave me their contact information and said I could call them anytime I wanted.) Debbie said he was the cutest little baby boy. Then she asked me when we would be able to come to Mississippi? I told her that I'd have to talk to Shawn, but that I was sure we could leave immediately as soon as we were packed. Debbie asked if we were flying, and we said no that we would be driving since we were bringing Myles with us.

Just as soon as I was off the phone with Debbie, I got on the phone with Shawn. I told him everything I had written down. He was so excited. I'm pretty sure we both cried, even though I can't remember for absolute sure. I asked Shawn about when he thought we could leave, and he said as soon as we got the van rented and packed, we could be on our way. I hung up with him, finalized my work to be gone for 3 months, then I made phone calls to family to relay our exciting news. Everyone was ecstatic for us. Then I left work as quickly as I could. I picked Myles up from Daycare and asked them to reserve a spot for our new son in the baby room following my three-month maternity leave. All the daycare teachers shared in my excitement. Myles and I got home before Shawn did, and I called the family to take care of the dogs. At this point in the day, I didn't have time to make reservations at the vet for boarding them because I was already running around the house like a chicken with its head cut off getting everything else ready to go. So we relied on our family to help with the dogs.

We had to plan on being gone from home for at least one week, possibly longer, depending on when we could finalize the adoption. I got all our suitcases packed and put them by the front door. The next thing I knew, Shawn was home with the rented van, all gassed up. He came into the house, took a shower, and then took the dogs over to our family. While he was gone, I got the van all packed up. As soon as Shawn got home, we called The Adkins to check on the baby and see how he was. We also let them know what our intentions were and when we planned to be there. Diane, the foster mother, answered in the sweetest-sounding southern accent and said the baby was doing just fine. Also, since he didn't come with a name, she had named him Joshua. I told Diane that was a nice name but that we intended on naming him something else, even though we hadn't yet finalized what it would be. She completely understood that we wanted to give him his name but in the meantime would continue to call him Joshua. As soon as I got off the phone with the Adkins, we locked up the house and left for Mississippi. It was about 7 pm by this time. We could not wait to meet our new baby boy!

Shawn drove all night. Myles slept in his car seat, and as much as I wanted to keep my eyes open to keep Shawn company while he drove, I just couldn't. I slept on and off all night. The only time we stopped was for gas, for drive-throughs for food, and to let Myles run around to burn off some pent-up energy. Shawn and I spent some of the time trying to figure out what our baby's name would be. Even though he wasn't absolutely crazy about the name Nelsyn...I was, and I more or less begged him to agree to name him that. Besides, the name we had chosen for a boy prior, Isaiah, didn't feel right anymore. It felt like it belonged to that baby we were going to adopt but it didn't work out. I ended up winning that battle. Nelsyn it was. Khaden would be his middle name, after his birth mother Kadenya.

It was a 14-hour drive to Coldwater, Mississippi, and we pulled into Gary and Diane's driveway at around 5 pm Wednesday afternoon. The Atkins' house was not at all what I had envisioned it would be. It was a huge brick home and very beautifully landscaped. It made me a little nervous when we pulled in because I thought maybe they would think we wouldn't be good enough for them, but boy were my premonitions wrong. Diane knew to expect us and had apparently been watching for us because she had met us in the driveway with our new baby in her arms. I could not unbuckle my seat belt and get out of the van fast enough. The very first time I saw him, I noticed how much he looked like Myles when he was a newborn! The resemblance was uncanny to me. This baby also had sleek black hair and fair skin. Diane had him loosely wrapped in a blanket as it was very warm. She placed him in my arms and said, "Hi y'all, I'm Diane and this is your new son." Diane was a middle-aged petite blond, short-haired woman. She was wearing a blossomy summer dress, no make-up, and was barefoot when she met us in the driveway. I could instantly tell she was a genuine soul. And her deep southern accent completed her ensemble. She gave off a warm feeling of welcome. Diane then said, "Y'all grab your bags if you want and come on in." We had no idea what to expect, let alone an invitation to stay at their home, while we waited for our baby's adoption to be finalized.

We walked in, and the first thing I noticed about their beautiful home was about 20 tomatoes ripening on their kitchen counter. I knew instantly that we were going to be just fine here and that they were normal people, in the midst of their huge home. When we walked into their open-floor-plan home, Gary was in the family room in his recliner, looking at his laptop and watching the news. He got up and shook our hands, then gave us a giant bear hug. Although quite a bit older than Diane, he had not a gray hair on his head. He had a jolly look to him with his rosy red cheeks, and a Southern accent as thick as his wife's. His welcoming gestures were just as warm as Diane's too. It was then that a wave of thankfulness came over me that our new son had been with these two extremely fine folks for the first seven days of his life.

We sat on their couch in the family room and unwrapped our new baby, counted his fingers and toes, gave him kisses, stroked his soft skin and sleek black hair, and admired how adorable and commented on how lanky he was. We held him close to us, took in his yummy newborn baby smell, and gave him more kisses. It was official, we were in love with him! Diane wondered if we had settled on a name for him yet, and we told her we had, and that his name would be Nelsyn. She looked at him and then back at us and said sure enough he looked just like a Nelsyn! After our initial bonding experience, Diane asked us if we wanted to see the nursery. Cradling him in my arms, I carried Nelsyn to the room that she introduced us to -- a room that was painted floor to ceiling in a gorgeous soft mural right out of the book, "Guess How Much I Love You," (by Sam McBratney, illustrated by Anita Jeram) complete with fluffy blue and white clouds for the sky and green grass at the bottom and a mural of Little Nutbrown Hare and his Father Big Nutbrown Hare. "I Love You to the Moon and Back" was stenciled on the wall above the hares. I thought surely I was dreaming. Near the ceiling were shelves that went all the way around the room. Sitting on the shelving were stuffed animals. All around the room were stuffed animals! There was a white crib, and a matching changing table and chest of drawers, a rocker glider, and a twin bed. This room truly looked like something you'd see in a home makeover magazine. It was picture-perfect and made me happy to know that Nelsyn had spent time in this cheerful room. Diane then said she and Gary had had over fifty foster babies in their time doing Foster Care! They were amazing, unselfish, beautiful people.

On one side of the nursery was a smaller bedroom with twin bunk beds. On the other side was a bathroom with tropical fish decor, and next to that was yet another bedroom, but larger with a queen bed and hunting decor. She said that was her son Trey's room. And this was just on one side of the house. There were two bathrooms, the master bedroom, and a dining room on the other half of the house, and upstairs there was a huge office and storage/play space. In their backyard was a beautiful brick patio, a man-made pond, and the biggest garden you ever seen. There was also a playground space and an old tree with a swing. Their house was large, yet very inviting. Diane and Gary offered for us to stay at their home while we finalized all the paperwork for the adoption. Since they had plenty of space and everything was set up for a baby, and they had made us feel so comfortable, it was an offer we couldn't refuse, so we absolutely 100% agreed to stay there. It was a no-brainer. Diane and Gary's hospitality were like the cherry on top of the adoption.

However, prior to arriving at the Adkins home, we had planned for Nana (Myles' birth grandmother) and Myles' birth mother, Ariana, to drive down from Atlanta so they could meet Nelsyn and we could all see each other again. We had thought though that we'd be in a hotel, not knowing we'd be invited to stay with the Adkins at their home. So, later that evening, I asked Diane if it would be okay for Nana and Ariana to come to their home to meet the new baby. She not only agreed, she offered them a room if they would want to spend the night...she said there was plenty of space in their home for everyone. I couldn't believe how open and comfortable and accommodating they were with us all being complete strangers. Maybe they saw something in us - the same thing we saw in them - family.

We got Myles all settled into the larger room where he slept in the same bed as Shawn, while I planned on sleeping in the nursery on the twin bed with Nelsyn. That first night with him was magical. I loved every minute I had with him. It was just the two of us, and even though I was exhausted from our trip, I gladly fed him, changed him, rocked him, and sang to him all night. I couldn't get enough of my new baby! I held him in my arms and thanked God for him, for our family that he had so marvelously put together.

I was comforted knowing that Nelsyn's birth mother had already relinquished her rights to him and that all we had to do was go before a judge and finalize the adoption. So when I did sleep, I slept soundly knowing everything was going to be okay. It was such a drastically different experience from Myles' adoption.

In the morning (Thursday), we contacted Debbie at New Beginnings to see what our next step was. She said they would contact the courthouse to see when the judge could get us in his chambers to finalize the adoption and then she would get back to us. Debbie said it would be a couple of days. So we decided to make and finalize plans for Nana and Ariana to come the next day. The rest of the day Thursday, we just lounged around and held Nelsyn and played outside with Myles. The weather was so hot and humid, more so than in Nebraska. There was a huge bullfrog that lived in their backyard pond, and it became Myles' mission to find it. (He never did though) We also got to meet Diane and Gary's children, Trey and Megan, and Megan's daughter, Abby. Abby was a couple of years older than Myles. In addition, we met the neighbors Dana and her daughter Annie. Diane called her Annie Belle, which I thought was so cute. Myles and Annie Belle were the same age and they got along so well. I think we got to see them every day that we were there. It was such a blessing for Myles to have a playmate because at the age of almost 4 years old, he needed someone to help keep him busy. What a wonderful relaxing day Thursday was.

The next morning, Nana and Ariana arrived. We hadn't seen Ariana since Myles was born, and it had been a couple of years since we last saw Nana, as she had made the trip to Nebraska a couple of years prior to seeing Myles when he was 18 months old. Nana was of course so happy to see Myles and us, but she was also very much ready to meet her new grandbaby. She held Nelsyn and cooed over him as every grandmother does when they first meet their grandchild. It was pretty special to see Ariana again, and we took lots of pictures. I can only imagine how it felt for Ariana to see Myles. While they were here, Ariana, Ms. Diane, and I went shopping while Nana and Shawn kept the boys. It was so great spending time with Ariana, and it felt so natural to be around her.

Nana and Ariana left late that next day. The following day, we were set to meet the judge to finalize Nelsyn's adoption. Ms. Diane drove us to the courthouse, and we all waited in the courtroom for the judge. When he arrived, he made us feel so comfortable, and he also acted excited for our new little family. He told us that adoptions were one of his favorite things to preside over since there was so much joy. He signed all the papers then asked if we wanted to keep the pen he used. It was official: Nelsyn was ours forever!

I had always kept Nelsyn's birth mother's name close to my heart. I thought if he ever got sick and we needed information on her, I would do anything in my power to find her, no matter if the adoption was closed or not. Well, come to find out, a couple of years later I searched for her by her name and found her on Facebook (It's not too hard to be found when you're the only one with that first name in that small town in Mississippi). I located her not because Nelsyn was sick or anything like that, but because I was curious as to what she looked like and wanted to be able to show Nelsyn if he ever asked. I couldn't believe I found her! Now what? I wanted so badly to connect with her, yet I totally respected her when she said she didn't want to keep in contact and have a closed adoption. However, a couple of months later, I finally got the nerve to send her a message on Facebook Messenger. On December 28, 2014, I wrote, "7/25/07. God bless you and yours this Christmas season. -- Angela." No response. I waited until almost two years later, on August 1, 2016, to send another message, "7/25/07. 9 years ago we received one of the best gifts ever. A son. God bless you. --Angela." No response. Again I waited approximately another 2 years, on May 13, 2018, to send the next one, "Dear Kadenya, we have an amazing someone in common, and even almost 11 years later, I want you to know how grateful I am and how often I thank God for you. Happy Mother's Day. Love, Angie Wheeler". Then on June 18, 2018, she responded! She wrote, "Hello, this is one of the most surreal moments. Playing with (Facebook) Messenger last night when I saw your message. There was a flood of a thousand emotions." I responded, "Oh my goodness...Hello!," "I can only imagine. That's how I felt when I finally found you. I was so nervous when I first reached out to you back in 2014. I have been patient knowing that if we were to ever connect, it would be in God's timing." She replied, "Knowing that it had to be God, bc I've thought about that little guy so much lately." "Angie I have to be completely honest with you, the (birth) dad has no idea Nelsyn survived birth. I told him I had a miscarriage. Giving my baby away was the hardest thing I've ever had to do, it has left an empty spot in my heart. When I looked at your (Facebook) page last night, he looked just like him, but I was so relieved that he has the chance to be nothing like him."

Even though that was the last time we communicated, I am forever grateful that we got to.

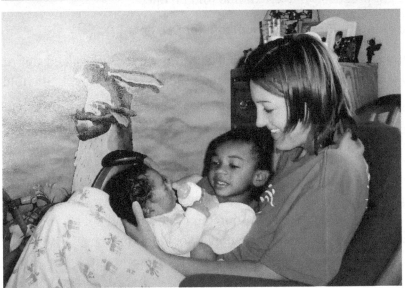

CHAPTER 4

She Cried

She was raped. She cried. She told no one.

She got pregnant. She cried. She told no one.

She chose abortion. She cried. She told no one.

She walked into abortion clinic. She was next. She walked out of abortion clinic. She chose life. She chose adoption. She cried. She told no one.

She chose us. She had a baby girl. She cried. I cried. Our baby cried. She told me everything.

For as long as I could remember, I had always wanted three children, just like my parents had, and subsequently just like Shawn's parents too. But now since we would be adopting our children, and not having them biologically, the plan was to just adopt two. And I had been completely fine with two ... until I wasn't. When Nelsyn was about 2 years old, I felt in my heart that I wanted to have another baby. And when you feel something in your heart like that, it's very hard to ignore. So one day, I broached Shawn about my thoughts, and he absolutely refused to even talk about it further, stating that not only had we agreed on just two children, but he never wanted to go through the adoption process ever again. Even though I wasn't happy with his reaction, I respected his decision and also didn't blame him one bit because adoption is an arduous and expensive ordeal. Instead of arguing with him, I just let it be. It was the hardest thing, but for a year, I intentionally didn't bring it up at all. In the meantime, I prayed feverously and faithfully, trusting that God was hearing my prayers. I prayed that if it was meant to be, Shawn would have a change of heart. I also prayed that if it wasn't meant to be, whatever these feelings were and wherever they were coming from would go away. The problem is not only did they not go away, they got stronger. A year later, I got up enough courage to ask him again. The answer was the same: No. I was so confused as to why God was not answering my prayers and not taking these feelings away if the answer was no. I had never felt so strongly about something before as I did about adopting again. Once more, I remained silent, but I never stopped praying.

Early Springtime 2010 my sister found out she was having twins! Instead of being genuinely happy for her, deep down, I was dying inside. I absolutely hate to admit it but it was jealousy. The sad kind of jealousy. The kind you don't want to be but can't control. I hated and felt absolutely horrible that I was jealous of her being pregnant. I loved her and her unborn babies so much, but all I wanted was another baby myself, and I had no other choice in the matter, and then here she was having two! I now admit that I had a hard time seeing her beautiful belly grow bigger as her pregnancy progressed. It was difficult for me to listen to her talk about the trials and joys of being pregnant. I had a hard time even being around her as every time I saw her, I was reminded that the answer for me was "no" when the answer for her was "yes." No one, not even Shawn, knew of this painful jealousy. However, my parents were aware of the desires of my heart to adopt again. One day, they stopped by our house to bring something by, and I remember out of the blue just blurting out to them that it (adopting again) was never going to happen, that Shawn still wasn't for it, and that I was trying my hardest to be respectful of his decision. What I was actually doing at that moment was going through the process of admitting defeat. Maybe if I said it out loud that would help?

That summer, we were camping with our family and I could see how much my sister's babies had been growing (how big her belly already was getting). Upon seeing this, I felt a terrible emptiness inside. A couple of minutes later, with tears in my eyes, I went to the campground showers and I stood under that shower for a good hour just crying my eyes out and feeling sorry for myself that I would never have another child.

The twins were born two days after Christmas. It seriously was all I could do to go to the hospital to see them. Instead of me being the genuinely happy and supportive older sister and proud aunt to these two beautiful babies, inside it was as if I was slowly melting in my own sorrow. Today I still feel guilty that I had ever felt this way towards her pregnancy. I love my sister and her children very much!

Although I never stopped praying, another year passed by with not a single mention to Shawn about adopting again. Then, one afternoon, it hit me hard. Those feelings. I was sitting on the front porch with tears streaming down my face. Shawn had been mowing, and upon seeing I was upset, he stopped and asked me what was the matter. Bawling, I was completely honest with him and told him how I had been begging God for two years to take these feelings away from me but how they had just gotten stronger and how I was trying my hardest to respect his decision but I didn't know how I was supposed to move on with this burden of not adopting again. There, I finally said it. I was really fearing his response, especially since it had been so long since I had brought this up. But no joke, after a brief pause, he looked me in the eyes and said, "It's obvious that we are supposed to do this because God is not taking these feelings away from you. If it's supposed to happen, God will find a way (financially)." Ummm, excuse me? I couldn't believe what I was hearing. Did he just say yes?! Throughout the past two years, not only had God heard my prayers, but He had answered them in his own timing and in his own way! My husband was completely serious when he said we could adopt again. It seemed as if, after all, God had planted a seed in Shawn, and my patience and prayers had paid off! Well, you can probably imagine the major excitement that ensued. "Thank you, God!!!" I whispered to myself. Then big hugs and kisses followed by a hundred "thank you's" to Shawn. I called all of our family to share the good news that we were going to have another baby!

Knowing we had a long road ahead of us—months of paperwork, meetings, etc.—I didn't waste a single moment to begin the adoption process. The next day, I contacted New Beginnings in Mississippi, the same agency we went through when we adopted Nelsyn. We had such an amazing experience with them that it was, of course, a no-brainer we would go through them again. They were thrilled to have us apply and mailed us the application. Next, I knew we needed to find an agency in Nebraska that would do our Home Study for us. We wanted to go through Roberta with Lutheran Family Services again, the case worker who completed our Home Study for Nelsyn. Instead of contacting Lutheran Family Services, I decided to contact Roberta directly. It didn't take me long to find Roberta on Facebook. I sent her a message through Messenger asking her if she would be willing to do another Home Study for us. We were delighted that she responded so quickly and, remembered us, and was happy to hear from us. Unfortunately, she said she was no longer with Lutheran Family Services and so was unable to assist with a Home Study. However, she instructed us to contact Lutheran Family Services, and they could provide us with some names of caseworkers who could help us. I did and was sent their paperwork with a list of names to contact.

Barbara was who we chose. The moment we met her, we knew we liked her a lot. Well into her seventies, she had been doing this for a long time. Barbara was the funniest person. She was not shy about anything and felt free to speak her mind whenever she wanted, and she did. She joked that we could probably do our own Home Study since this was our third time around the block. Barbara made us feel so comfortable. We went to her home to have our meetings, and then she came to our house once for the home visit. Soon, we had completed our Home Study. In the meantime, we began our application process through New Beginnings. The normal fingerprinting, financial rigmarole, background checks, mounds of paperwork, etc., followed. I would say it took us a good 3 months to get everything completed and into New Beginnings for processing. Soon after we turned it in, we got a notification that we were approved to move forward to adopt! That meant it was time for us to get our portfolio and Dear Birth Mom letter ready. As soon as we got that to them, we would be ready to be considered by birth mothers.

We gathered pictures of the four of us that would show a potential birth mother just how 'normal and worthy' of a family we were to adopt her baby. We labored over the Dear Birth Mom letter, wanting it to be a perfect representation of our family. Times have changed even in the 6 years since we adopted Nelsyn. Now, instead of a bound booklet for our portfolio, we were expected to make actual books (like Shutterfly books) and provide several copies to distribute throughout the adoption agency. The more copies we made, the more birth mothers would get a chance to see them. I think we made like 6 books. At this point, the cost of them didn't really matter too much to us as we had just wanted our portfolio to be viewed by as many potential birth mothers as possible. We were told that when we were chosen, most likely the birth mother would also want to keep a copy. That was fine with us. We made our books with a picture of the four of us on the front cover titled "The Wheelers," and this is what the Dear Birth Mom letter said:

Hello from Nebraska!

We are Shawn, Angela, Myles, and Nelsyn, and we are excited to be adding to our family! We are writing this letter to ask you to consider us for one of the most important decisions you'll ever make. This is coming straight from our hearts and it is being sent with admiration and appreciation for you. Adopting again is prayer's answer and really is a dream come true for our family.

When a husband and wife decide to have children, it is because they have a God-given desire to be parents, to love their children, provide for them, and nurture them. It's the exact same with Shawn and me. We so badly wanted to be parents when we were first married. We tried and tried to have a child. Finally, six years later, we accepted that if we were going to have the family we always wanted, we'd be taking a different route to achieve this. That's when God planted adoption in our hearts (we never looked back!). Fast forward ten years and we now have two incredible sons and are hoping for our third child—all through the gift of adoption.

Once, someone told us that we had done such a good thing by adopting the boys and that they were so lucky to have us for parents. Well, that's not at all what our adoption story has been about. It's never been about us wanting to do a good thing; rather, it's been about us wanting to have and be a real family. Lucky? No. We are BLESSED! We all are."

Adding to our family is something we want very much and have been excited about for a long time now. The love we feel for our boys is so natural and incredible, there are no words to describe it, and we have already fallen in love with this new little one that we haven't even met yet! Boy or girl? Doesn't matter to us one bit. Yes, it would be fun to experience a daughter, but we would be just as thrilled with another son!

You may or may not be considering having an open adoption with the family you choose. We have experience with both because although we do have an open relationship with Myles' birth family, we do not with Nelsyn's. We will respect any decision you make. However, if an open adoption is what you wish for, please know we are absolutely willing to have one with you.

Giving honor and recognition to the women who have given birth to our children is something we do regularly in our home. It is extremely important for our sons to know that their birth mothers loved them so much -- that they not only gave them life but also a future. Every night when we say our prayers, we thank God for our birth mothers and for the plan He had for us to become a family.

Thank you for reading our letter and considering our family. No matter where you go from here, you've already made the best decision by choosing life for your baby. We appreciate that so much. We pray you will experience peace, comfort, reassurance, courage, and healing in the choices you make for your child and yourself.

Sincerely,

Shawn, Angela (Myles and Nelsyn too!)

We give thanks for unknown blessings already on their way.

--Anonymous

I mailed our portfolio books to New Beginnings in April of 2013. We were officially in the running to adopt!

We were confident that we'd get chosen eventually, but we also knew it might take some time since this was our third adoption, and sometimes, birth mothers choose families that have no prior children first. While we waited to be chosen, we kept busy with our boys, then nine and a half and almost six years old. Shawn also had been working hard to transform the playroom in the basement into a bedroom for the boys, and after that, he worked on getting the boys' old bedroom upstairs transformed into a nursery for the baby. I bought unisex clothing and stocked the baby changing table full of diapers of all sizes wipes, and anything else you could think of for a newborn. Fresh paint and a crib borrowed from my sister. I then took over the decorating. The theme we chose was The Very Hungry Caterpillar by Eric Carle. A couple of final touches and the nursery was ready. Before we knew it, the boys were both back in school, Myles in 4th grade and Nelsyn in Kindergarten. Summer was officially over.

August came and went, and then the first Thursday in September when I was at work, a call came in from the adoption agency. It was THE CALL we had waited for! A baby boy was due anytime, and the birth mother had chosen our family! To say I was excited was an understatement! I couldn't believe we were getting another boy! That was absolutely perfect for us because that's all we knew - boys. I immediately called Shawn, and we decided not to tell anyone else in our family until we told the boys that night after we got home. I got everything ready at work to be gone for an extended period. Shawn did the same. That same afternoon, we actually received a text with a picture of the birth mom, Brittany. She was so beautiful and so brave to have made an adoption plan for her unborn child! And her sending us a picture of her was an excellent sign that she was serious about following through with this. I went to the bank after work and withdrew some of the cash we had saved for the adoption. I didn't know who the bank teller was, but it didn't matter one bit. Overcome with excitement, I showed her the picture of the birth mother and told her we were getting a baby! Of course, she was happy for us but was probably thinking I was looney for showing her (more or less a complete stranger) a picture of the birth mother. I didn't care; I wanted to shout it out to the world that I was about to become a mommy again!

That night at the supper table, we told the boys about the baby. Of course, the only thing they were really actually excited about was that they'd get to go to The Great Wolf Lodge, like we had already told them we'd do when we adopted again. Shawn gave the boys fresh haircuts. Later on, when they were in the bathtub, I was talking to my parents on the phone and telling them our good news. Mom asked me to put her on speaker so she could talk to the boys while I was bathing them. She and Dad asked them if they were excited, and Nelsyn said, "Did you hear the good news, Papa? We're getting another brother!" It was the sweetest thing. I spent the rest of the evening getting all of our bags packed, including the babies.

The next day was Friday, and we went to work as usual since there was no point in using vacation days until we actually needed them, and besides, the baby hadn't been born yet anyway. The day went by slowly. Around supper time, we received notice that the birth mother had gone into labor, and we had better head out. Since we had already packed everything and had been to the bank, we were able to just put everything into the van and take off. We left at about 7:00 pm. We had a long drive ahead of us, at least fifteen or so hours, which included stops. We estimated we'd be there by around 2 pm the following day. Hopefully, the boys would fall asleep as soon as it got dark and sleep most of the night. Sure enough, about 9 pm, they both fell fast asleep. We had already decided on names for both a boy and a girl. Pehrsyn if it was a boy and Paelyn if it was a girl. Pehrsyn's middle name would be *Britton* after his birth mother's name, Brittany. Now that we had the baby named, we waited for any news from Jody, the case worker who was assigned to us.

Around 1 am, the phone rang. It's not like we were expecting a call from anyone else besides Jody at that hour; however, my stomach still did a flip-flop when I saw that it was her. Shawn was driving, so I answered. She said hello to us and asked us how our trip was going. I told her it was good that the boys were sleeping. Next, all in the same breath, she told us, "The baby had been born, but the birth mother was 'on the fence' about the adoption plan." 'On the fence,' what was she trying to tell us? "What do you mean she's 'on the fence'?" I asked. She explained that ever since he had come into this world (and he actually was born at 9 pm), she had been having second thoughts about giving him up. I felt like I had been punched in the gut. Like the joy I had been feeling came to a crashing halt. I couldn't believe what I was hearing. I covered up the receiver and whispered to Shawn what I had been told. I got back on the phone, "So what should we do now?" I asked.

Jody explained that in these situations, which happen a lot once a baby is born, it is best for the adoptive family to come as planned since there is still a good chance that the Birth Mother would continue through with the adoption, but that it was up to us if we wanted to take that risk or not. I told Jody we'd have to talk about it and call her back. I got off the phone and relayed to Shawn the rest of what Jody had told me. I looked at him and started to cry. He asked me what I thought we should do? I said, "What if he is supposed to be ours and Jody is right and she does go through with it?" I told Shawn we would never know if we didn't try. He said, "But what about all this money on gas and food and hotels we're spending if it doesn't work out?"

We both thought for a moment then came to the same consensus: we would continue on with our trip to Mississippi and pray for the best. That's exactly what I did. I prayed. This was like one of the worst-case scenarios that could happen with an adoption. I prayed for God's will to be done, but then I found myself arguing with God. Why would He allow us to go through it? We had been faithful with our prayers, so why was this happening? Why us? It was surreal. Every time I thought of Pehrsyn, my stomach ached. I had fallen in love with that baby. I ached for that baby. And now I didn't know if I was going to get that baby. What was I thinking? He wasn't even mine yet. She (his birth mother) had every right to him. Who was I to call him my child?

Shawn drove the rest of the night, and I dozed off and on, each time waking up to the reality of our nightmare. During the night, we had decided we were going to tell the boys right away when they woke up so they could mentally prepare themselves instead of having to deal with it later. Day broke, and the boys woke up. Crap, how were they supposed to understand this? Gently, I told them what happened while they had been sleeping. I told them we might not be getting a new brother. They had questions, and we answered them the best we could. Nelsyn started crying, and before long, he was throwing a huge fit. "Why are we on this stupid trip anyway if we don't even get to keep him!?" he screamed.

I calmed him down and tried to sugarcoat the situation and brighten up the mood and sound positive like it wasn't a big deal at all. I told him that even though we didn't know if we were going to get a baby, we were still going to continue our trip to Mississippi and we'd still see Ms. Diane, and we'd still go to the Great Wolf Lodge. That seemed to satisfy him for the moment. Myles was quiet and seemed almost too mature for his age, like he completely understood what was going on. These poor boys of ours.

As soon as I thought it wasn't too early, about 8 am, I called Jody to see if she had any good news for us. She told us that nothing had really changed except that Brittany still wanted to meet with us. I was so confused. "Why would she want to meet us if she was on the fence?" I asked. Jody responded that this could be a good sign that she still might be leaning towards adoption, but that only time would tell. For the first time in hours, I felt hope in my bones. Hope that this was actually going to turn out good. We knew she had 72 hours before she could sign relinquishment. We could do this. I mean, my gosh, we did it for 12 days when we adopted Myles; this would be a walk in the park. We made arrangements with Jody to meet at 4 pm at the hospital. That would give us enough time to get settled at Ms. Diane's, freshen up, and then get there by 4. I then called Ms. Diane and told her what was happening. She said she was so sorry we were going through all this, but she was sure getting excited to see us all.

We made it to Ms. Diane's at around 2:00 pm. She had already planned to take Myles and Nelsyn to her granddaughter's soccer game with her, so we wouldn't have to take them with us. That was the last thing we needed to deal with – the boys while we were meeting the birth mother. Ms. Diane was such a saint! We unpacked our bags, and then Shawn and I took badly needed showers. We were both covered in grief, road trip, and sleeplessness and wanted to make sure we looked fresh and hopefully make the best first impression we could. Shawn and I left the boys in the capable hands of Ms. Diane and headed to the hospital. On the 45-minute drive, we giddily talked about Pehrsyn as if he was already ours. We were definitely hopeful.

As soon as we got into town, we called Jody to tell her we were almost at the hospital. She said to meet her outside the Admissions Entrance. We arrived, parked, and got out of our vehicle. There standing outside was a woman in what had to be her mid-twenties. I just knew it was her. I asked her if she was Jody at the same time she asked us if we were The Wheelers. We all said yes then gave each other hugs. Even though we had never met her in person, we felt like she was an old friend. Jody led us inside, then pulled us aside and told us matter-of-factly, without a hint of emotion, that Brittany had decided to parent her baby. The first thing I thought was, "Why were we even there then?" She told us that she still wanted to meet us, though.

Now, this was something I didn't understand at all. But we said okay and had no choice but to keep our composure and followed Jody down to a hall of hospital rooms. She knocked on one of the doors, and we heard a woman's voice telling us to come in. We entered after Jody, and there lying in a hospital bed was Brittany, very recognizable from the picture that was previously sent to us. Across from her was a man. I looked around; there was no baby in sight. Jody introduced us to Brittany, and we shook her hands. She then introduced us to the man and said this was the baby's father. Jody asked Brittany if she wanted to tell us what she had decided to name her baby? She told us, but I can't remember exactly what it was, even though I do recall it starting with a Z. My heart was breaking, but I kept it together. We swallowed the lump in our throats and told her congratulations, and then an awful silence ensued. Not knowing why we were even there, even though I realized later on this was all an important part of the grieving process for us,

55

Shawn finally broke the silence and offered to say a prayer. We all held hands while Shawn thanked God for this new life. I couldn't stand it a minute longer, I had to get out of there. We said our goodbyes and best wishes, and then Jody led us back out to the waiting room. Although she was one of the kindest people you'll ever meet, Jody was very unapologetic about the situation. Not that this was her fault and that she needed to apologize at all, but what we needed then was somebody to acknowledge our feelings, our hurts.

But I'm sure this was part of her training and she knew what was best for us at that moment. Jody asked us what our plans were. I couldn't think straight. We told her we'd maybe stay with Ms. Diane for a couple of days, then take the boys to the Great Wolf Lodge in Kansas City on our way home. There was no point in us staying in Mississippi any longer than we needed to because we shouldn't be wasting our vacation time since we would eventually be adopting again in the future, right? We thanked Jody for everything, hugged her, and she told us she was looking forward to seeing us the next time (we would be there to adopt).

We got into the car, and both of us burst into tears. There was no exchange of words; we just held each other and wept. Then I stopped crying, and I told Shawn that we had to get to the boys!

Suddenly, all I could think about was our boys and how I had to protect them from this hurt that we were experiencing! It was the oddest feeling of a mother fiercely wanting to protect her children. I then got mad, mad at myself that we had even gotten so involved in this adoption. We should have known better not to tell the boys, let alone call him their brother and name him! Shawn agreed we needed to go see the boys. Then he looked at me and of course, had the perfect thing to say at that moment. He said, "You know, it's probably a good thing this didn't work out because did you see that birth father? He was uggggly, and we can't have an ugly kid." We both laughed so hard at that. (Of course, the birth father wasn't that bad-looking at all, but Shawn knew just what to say to cheer me up). We dried our tears and then drove off. I began to call our family to let them know what had happened and our new change of plans. It was such a sorrowful time for Shawn and me. We got back to Ms. Diane's at suppertime. To say we were exhausted is an understatement. We were drained on all fronts. Not only from the all-night trip to Mississippi but the emotional day that followed. I could barely keep my eyes open. We ate, gave the boys a bath, then put them to bed in one of Ms. Diane's guest bedrooms. The door to her beautiful nursery was shut and served as a reminder of our loss. As soon as the boys went to sleep, Shawn and I went to bed ourselves, even though it was only like 8:00 pm. I don't remember falling asleep, and I don't think I moved at all that night. I slept long and hard.

The next morning I awoke to our new reality. The sorrow hit again once more, and the tears did, too. I noticed I had some missed calls on my cell phone. One was from my Grandma Keown, and she left a long message about how sorry she was that this was all happening but that God was still good and had a good plan for us, etc. The thing she said that really got me was this, "And honey, God doesn't make mistakes." Wow. What a different way to look at this situation. I could feel my spirits lift, and this truth gave me the courage to move on and to look forward to the future. We would be getting a baby, just not this time. We stayed with Ms. Diane another night. Before we went to bed, we packed all of our bags into the van. Early the next morning, we gave hugs and said our goodbyes and our thank-yous to Ms. Diane and promised we'd see her again, hopefully very soon (when we adopted again). We needed to leave early because we had a long drive ahead of us to get to Kansas City before nightfall. The trip there was uncomfortable, to say the least. You could feel the thick sorrow in the air, and that mixed with two little boys who had just lost a brother yet were overly excited to go to The Great Wolf Lodge - it was all a little much.

But I had to admit that I was also excited to go to The Great Wolf Lodge too as I knew we'd have much-needed fun and relaxation. We would try our hardest to make this into a positive trip for our boys, which meant we'd need to set aside our sorrows. The Great Wolf Lodge did not disappoint and was exactly what our family needed. Myles was old enough to go exploring in the lodge by himself, while Nelsyn spent most of his time swimming. We mini-golfed and played in the arcade. Across the street was a Russell Stover outlet store, and I'm telling you I ate my feelings that weekend in so much chocolate and ice cream. The Great Wolf Lodge was a happy place that allowed us to temporarily escape the sadness. Soon, though, it was time to end our mini-vacation and get back to reality. We'd have to face our friends and families and the people at work with empty arms. We got home Tuesday afternoon and dove right back into life on Wednesday... without Pehrsyn. Boy was that hard. But it was time to move on and look forward to our next chance to adopt. I called New Beginnings later that day to make sure our profile was still out there for potential birth mothers to see, and they reassured me it was.

That Friday I was supposed to go on an overnight work retreat, but I just couldn't bring myself to go. We were still grieving over our failed adoption. When the big boss didn't understand where I was coming from, my boss Donna came to my rescue and vouched for me that my husband and I needed this time to heal. I was then excused from the retreat. Thankfully the Holidays were coming upon us, so that kept our minds busy while we patiently waited for the next adoption call. Around Christmas, I got a little antsy and began to wonder if we needed to change our portfolio. Maybe the picture on the front, which had been just a snapshot of the four of us together, wasn't a good enough one. I decided we'd get our family pictures professionally taken and use one of them to update the cover of our portfolio books. That'd mean we'd need to order all-new books. We didn't care about the cost; we just wanted something fresh and new for the birth mothers to look at.

So on a very frigid December afternoon, we had our family pictures taken outdoors by a bridge. I felt much better having a professional new look to our portfolio. We mailed the new books and asked them to dispose of the old ones. Christmas came and went, and then January hit. January was long and cold, and we did not hear a word from the adoption agency. When February arrived, I began to give up hope that this was ever going to happen. It was the beginning of the week, and I was at work, and all I could think of that day was that I was done with all of this. I was tired of waiting. I didn't think I could walk by the empty nursery in our home another day. I couldn't keep waiting for a phone call. I was just absolutely done with it all. We'd call the adoption agency and have them pull our portfolio. We'd turn the nursery into an office. I wanted to tell Shawn how I felt, and I would as soon as we both got home. That was Monday.

For some reason, and even though my feelings were still strong that I wanted to surrender, I never did tell Shawn how I felt that night.

It was late Wednesday afternoon, the absolute coldest, iciest day so far that year. I had just gotten back from a meeting. I was sitting at my desk when the phone rang. I recognized the number. It was New Beginnings. Oh my gosh. Could it really be? I answered, and it was Debbie. She relayed to me that we had been chosen by a birth mother who was due to have a baby girl any day now! And would we be interested? I could hardly believe what I was hearing. Just a couple of days earlier, I was ready to pull the plug on all this adoption stuff, and now here I was getting the phone call we'd been waiting for since April! I told her absolutely yes, we would be interested! Debbie gave me some details. The birth mother's name was Quaniyah. She was in the early stages of labor, which meant we needed to leave right now. (I said we'd leave as soon as we could.) Debbie told me that we could talk more details later on the phone when we were on the road, but that we better get moving. I got off the phone with her and was literally squealing with delight. I told my coworkers that we were going to have a baby girl very soon, and I had to leave right away.

Thankfully I was prepared, so all I had to do was update my Out of Office Assistant that I was going to be on maternity leave. But before I left, I called Shawn to tell him the news. He also agreed that we needed to leave right away, especially since she was already in labor. I told him I'd pick up the boys from Daycare then meet him at home.

On the way to Daycare, I called my parents to relay our news. They were ecstatic for us, but at the same time, they were very wary about us doing this again. What if it didn't turn out like last time? I said, but what if it did turn out? I told them we couldn't be afraid to take a risk, and there would never be a 100% guarantee. They understood but just didn't want our hearts to get broken again like they were when we lost out on baby Pehrsyn just months before.

When I got to Daycare, I told the teachers, and everyone was again, like they were before, so excited for us. I said we'd need them to hold a spot in the Baby Room for our new daughter when I got done with my maternity leave. Daughter. I liked the sound of that. Holy cow, I was going to have a daughter! We got home, and Shawn had already taken the dogs to my sister's house and had the van all packed. All we needed to do now was to change our clothes, grab our winter gear, and hit the road.

We got on the road at about 5 pm. The boys were hungry, so we went through the Wendy's drive-thru on the way out of town. It was still extremely cold and very icy, so we weren't able to drive at the speed limit. Then before long, the sun went down. We had a long, dark journey ahead of us. As soon as we were all settled in for the drive (the boys' tummies full and a movie playing on the DVD player), I called Debbie back. The first thing we wanted to know was how the birth mother was feeling. Debbie said she was doing just fine. I told her that we weren't able to drive at the speed limit because of the dangerous driving conditions, but that we'd hope to soon get into normal conditions the farther south we drove. I asked Debbie if the birth mother was still planning on adoption.

She reassured me she was very firm with her decision. I told her I was sorry I asked, but that we were just really nervous because of what happened last time. Debbie was very understanding, and I could hear confidence in her voice regarding this situation. She then gave us the phone number of the case worker who was working directly with the birth mother. Her name was Olevia. We would need to reach out to her with all of our questions from here on out, and she'd be able to help us and keep us updated as the birth mother's labor progressed. I thanked Debbie profusely for everything she had done for us already. She said she would see us very soon.

I contacted Olevia. She said she was right there with the birth mother and that she wouldn't be leaving her side. I was relieved to hear that, and glad to know that she would have a support system. I asked Olevia more questions, one of them being if the birth mother was interested in an open adoption? She answered back that she was not, that this was going to more or less be a closed adoption after it was all over with. We totally would respect her wishes, but of course, that is not what we were hoping for, yet what other choice did we have? I asked her how to spell the birth mother's name, and she told me it was Q u i n i y a h. I can't remember all the other questions I asked her, even though I know there were a lot. I got off the phone with Olevia with the promise that she'd keep in touch if anything changed with Quiniyah's labor.

Shawn and I spent the next hour or so working on a middle name for Paelyn, the first name we had decided on months before if it were to be a girl. We were trying to come up with a creative middle name after the birth mother's first name, but finally, when we weren't able to, we agreed on just Paelyn Quiniyah. That was a beautiful name. Good, so now that was settled. After that, we just drove and waited to hear any news from Olevia.

The boys fell asleep about 11, and before long, I couldn't keep my eyes open either. As I was dozing off, the phone rang. It was Olevia. She said that Quiniyah was now dilated to 3 and that things were progressing at a normal rate and that she was doing well. That news definitely woke me up. After we got off the phone, I texted our family to give them an update. And I prayed for Quiniyah to have strength and courage and pain-free labor. Then it was back to driving. We heard from Olevia a couple more times throughout the night, but by the time we got to St. Louis at 4 am, neither Shawn nor I could hardly keep our eyes open. It was getting dangerous, and we didn't want Shawn falling asleep at the wheel, so we decided to stop and sleep a while. Being in St. Louis at 4 am meant we needed to find a safe place to rest. We decided on the well-lit parking of a Cracker Barrel restaurant. Even though they were closed at that hour, we still felt safe since it was so lit up. We parked close to the entrance of the restaurant, locked the doors, then drifted off to sleep. We had to leave the van running since it was so cold outside. An hour later we woke up feeling so much better and alert. We then continued our drive.

At about the time we woke up from our little snooze, the phone rang. Olevia asked us where we were because Quiniyah was fully dilated and getting ready to deliver. Oh my goodness, talk about exciting! We told her we were in St. Louis, still seven hours away. She understood but told us to get there as quickly as we could. That news and the hour's worth of sleep we just got was just what we needed to push forward. We stopped at a McDonald's drive-thru, got some coffee, and continued on with the drive. At 6:03 am, we got a call that Quiniyah had given birth via emergency c-section. Both mom and baby were doing well, and Quiniyah was in recovery. Then we received a picture of our new daughter. She was all swaddled up with a big bow on her tiny little head. Paelyn was absolutely beautiful, and we just could hardly wait to hold her! (Even though we missed her birth, we didn't feel bad, especially since we weren't there for the births of our other two children.)

We finally arrived at the hospital at 11 am. We called Olevia to tell her we were there but said we needed to change our clothes first. We found a spot in the parking garage that was fairly deserted, and then we changed our clothes in the van. At this point, we could really care less if anyone saw us because after the long trip we had just been on, all we cared about was seeing our baby! The four of us entered the hospital, got onto the elevator, and up we went to the maternity floor. I had butterflies in my stomach. I was so nervous to meet Quiniyah. We got to the maternity floor and called Olevia to meet us in the lobby. Shortly thereafter, Olevia walked in. We greeted her with hugs and thank-yous for all that she had done for all of us so far. She led us to the hospital room where Quiniyah had just arrived after being in the recovery room following her c-section. We entered the room, and there she was in her hospital bed, drowsy still from the anesthesia, yet awake. I looked around but there was no baby. Olevia introduced us as The Wheelers, and we shook hands with Quiniyah. Quiniyah was a very pretty woman in her late 20s, with huge beautiful eyes and full lips.

She was pretty short, around 5 ft tall, and she had the tiniest feet on a grown woman that I'd ever seen before in my life. Although she was petite, her facial features were anything but. I asked her how she was feeling, and she responded that she wasn't really feeling anything yet, but was sure she'd be having pain as soon as the meds wore off. I wanted to ask her how she was feeling emotionally and if she still planned on making an adoption plan for her daughter, but I thought it better not to.

It was way too soon. Thankfully, the boys were both very quiet and well-behaved. I think they were taking in all that was happening as much as a 10 and 6-year-old could understand. We exchanged the usual niceties: "How was your trip?" "How was your night?" We told them how we slept for an hour in the parking lot of a Cracker Barrel with the van running, she told us why she had to have a c-section (I want to say it was because the baby's heart rate had dropped? But I can't recall for sure). Even though we wanted to know everything about her, we didn't ask any more questions about the baby since she wasn't even in the room. Plus we wanted to make sure that Quiniyah felt valued to us as a person, we didn't want to sound like all we cared about was the baby.

About 45 minutes into our visit, there came a knock at the door. In walked a nurse pushing a bassinet. Of course, lying inside the bassinet was the most beautiful baby girl in the world. She was even more adorable in person than she was in the photo. I just wanted to scoop her up in my arms, but I waited. Again, we didn't want to give the impression that all we cared about was the baby, besides we really had no rights to her yet. At this point, we were just visitors. The nurse left, and Quiniyah asked if we wanted to hold her? No doubt the answer was emphatically "Yes, please!" I walked over to the bassinet and scooped the baby into my arms. I just stood there cradling her with Shawn looking over my shoulders. I was in love. My time with her was short-lived because Myles and Nelsyn wanted to hold her, too. They each took a turn, with us helping Nelsyn while he held her. We all treated her as if she were a china doll, like one small move would break her into pieces. Then it was Shawn's turn to hold her. Once he was done, we didn't know if I was supposed to keep holding her or if Quiniyah wanted to, so we offered Paelyn to her. She said this was the first time she had a chance to really look at her. She made a comment about how beautiful she was, and we all agreed. I remarked about how tiny her nose was and how long her fingers were. She also had soft shiny black hair that was wrapped up in a giant bow. The baby was absolutely perfect.

Minutes later, Quiniyah was done holding her. I don't know if it was because her incision site began to hurt or if she was just trying to limit access to her baby, knowing the more she held her, the harder it would be to relinquish her. We re-swaddled her, and instead of me holding her like I was dying to do, I put her back in her bassinet. Before long, the boys became antsy, and Shawn and I decided they'd better go get something to eat and then head to the hotel to let the boys swim. Shawn and I seemed to naturally work together in perfect harmony that day, each playing the role we needed to at the moment. Me with the birth mom and baby, and he with the children. In fact, I ended up staying at the hospital until 7 pm while Shawn took care of the boys. After Shawn, Myles, and Nelsyn left, Quiniyah and I talked. She asked us what we were planning on naming her, and I told her Paelyn Quiniyah, as we had also given our boys middle names after their birth mother's first name. She was very quick to decline us using her first name for the middle name. (Now I know it was due to privacy issues.) I asked her if she had any ideas for a middle name, and she said that if she was going to keep her, she would have named her Maliyah. I then said, "What if we named her Paelyn Maliyah then"? She agreed that would be a nice name. Then I asked her why she chose us to be the adoptive family? She said she had seen the cover photo of our portfolio and thought, "That momma is surrounded by boys, and she needs a girl!" This made my heart smile.

I held and fed Paelyn the whole time I was there, from around noon until 7, only stopping to change her. I wanted to begin bonding with her as soon as possible, getting her used to my smell and my voice. Quiniyah and I would talk, and then she would suddenly fall asleep. This would occur on and off all afternoon. Of course, she had to have been so mentally, emotionally, and physically exhausted from her long night without so much as a wink of sleep. So, I would just sit there by myself and stare at this beautiful baby girl I was holding. However, sometimes I too, found myself not being able to keep my eyes open, so then I'd sleep when Quiniyah slept, all the while holding Paelyn. Around 7:00 pm, exhaustion was hitting me hard, and I was overly ready to see my husband and boys. Plus, I was also famished as I hadn't eaten anything since that morning. So, I called Shawn and asked him to pick me up. I said my goodbyes to Quiniyah, kissed Paelyn, then left the room with the promise that we'd return first thing in the morning, and that she could call us at any time. At that moment, I felt very confident that this adoption was going to turn out in our favor. That night, even though I felt really good about everything, I didn't sleep well at all. I found myself staring at the clock just waiting for morning to arrive.

The next morning, which was Friday, we got up, showered, ate breakfast, and then all headed back to the hospital to see Quiniyah and Paelyn. We got there at about 10:00. When we arrived at her hospital room, it was empty... Before we got a chance to panic, Olevia caught us in the hall and told us that Quiniyah had changed rooms because of privacy issues. What privacy issues? She said that when she originally had checked into the hospital, she requested to be on the private "unlisted" part of the directory so that if anyone called in to ask what room she was in, the hospital staff would say they didn't have anyone listed by that name.

However, somehow Quiniyah found out that her name was indeed listed on the hospital directory. Not only that, her name had been on the sign outside her hospital room and was also on the baby's bassinet. So, to be on the safe side, she changed rooms and was given an alias, Tora Blankly, which was then listed on the outside of her new room and also the baby's bassinet. So why such a need to keep things private? That wasn't revealed until later the next night.

We found her in her new hospital room, and we spent the rest of Friday morning taking turns holding Paelyn and talking to Quiniyah. She told us that Paelyn had spent the night in the nursery so she could get some rest. Secretly, I was relieved to hear this because I thought for sure the more time Quiniyah spent with Paelyn, the harder it would be for her to relinquish her parental rights after the 72 hours were up. Right before lunch, Nana arrived (from Stone Mountain, Georgia). We were all very excited to see her. We all hugged her then introduced her to Quiniyah. It had been over 4 years since we last were all together. Nana planned to stay until Sunday afternoon. She brought with her several bags full of new clothes for Paelyn. Nana was already spoiling Paelyn, and she wasn't even 2 days old yet! It was so fun opening each bag and oohing and aahing over the contents. One outfit was a Hello Kitty-themed open-ended gown with matching hat. It was adorable, and even though it was a newborn size, it was still a little too big for Paelyn. But

I didn't care, I planned on putting it on her when we brought her home from the hospital.

We left for lunch, and Nana stayed with Quiniyah and Paelyn. It was a good opportunity for them to chat and for Nana to empathize with what Quiniyah was going through, as her own daughter had also gone through placing a child (our Myles) for adoption. We thought that Nana would be good for Quiniyah to have in her life at that moment. When we returned from lunch, Nana took the boys back to the hotel to go swimming and give us some alone time to spend with Quiniyah. Thank goodness for Nana at this time! We ended up staying in the hospital room with Quiniyah and Paelyn until about 9:30 that evening. I was exhausted. We all were exhausted. When we got back to the hotel room, we put the boys to bed. I got ready for bed, and the next thing I knew, Shawn was putting his coat on. I asked him where he was going, and he said he was going back to the hospital to spend the night, and that someone needed to stay with Quiniyah so she wouldn't be alone. Plus, he wanted to take care of Paelyn instead of her being in the nursery. My heart was so thankful for such a good man and daddy to our children.

The next morning, Saturday, Shawn came back to the hotel, showered, and then we all went to the hospital. The end of the 72 hours, before she could sign relinquishment was, thank God, nearing. Quiniyah was holding Paelyn when we walked into her room. Shortly thereafter, there was a knock at the door and in came a Social Worker. She asked us to leave so she could talk to Quiniyah in private. Quiniyah said we could stay, but the Social Worker insisted we leave, so we did what was asked of us. While we were out of the room, we went to the McDonalds that was connected to the hospital and had some breakfast. We went back to Quiniyah's room after about thirty minutes thinking that probably was enough time for her and the Social Worker to talk, and if not, we would just wait in the hall for them to be done. They were finished, and what Quiniyah told us blew us away. She said that the purpose of the visit from the Social Worker was for her to try and talk Quiniyah out of placing her baby for adoption, convincing her that Paelyn was best off staying with her. But Quiniyah told the Social Worker she was firm about her decision and once she made up her mind, she didn't change it. She was just as annoyed at the Social Worker's visit as we were. She sounded dead serious, too. Whew, what a relief to actually hear her say it.

That afternoon Nelsyn was being quite antsy and acting naughty so both Shawn and Nana left with the boys to go swimming at the hotel. The plan was for me to spend the night with Quiniyah and Paelyn.

Quiniyah and I spent the afternoon holding, feeding, changing, and doting over Paelyn. We talked about anything and everything. Our friendship was blossoming, and I was becoming a safe person for her. I spilled it all—telling her about our infertility years, the boys' adoptions, and the adoption that didn't go through in September. She told me a little more about herself and her son.

Then she finally told me why she had switched hospital rooms. Come to find out, Quiniyah's mother and aunt had called around to all the local hospitals in Mississippi to find out which one she could be at and finally found her...room number and all. They then texted her they were coming. I was like, "OH MY GOSH, what?" I held onto Paelyn extra tight knowing there was nothing I could have done or said to stop them from taking her from us as Quiniyah was in no condition mentally, emotionally, or physically to fight her mother. But Quiniyah had been quick to think and asked the hospital staff to take her name off the door outside her hospital room and change her name to a bogus name. (So that's why Tora Blankly was the name on the door—it made sense now) The final thing they did to make sure her mom and aunt would never find her was to change her to a different hospital room. I was panicking inside. The ruse Quiniyah so strategically orchestrated all these months could come crashing down on her, and where would that leave all of us? Without Paelyn for sure. We made sure the door stayed closed at all times, just in case they were lurking outside. God had been watching over us that day.

We conversed some more, and then out of nowhere, she blatantly said that Nelsyn needed a belt with his name on it. I didn't know what she meant, so I asked her. She said he needed a whooping for the way he had been acting. "Spare the rod, spoil the child" (Proverbs 13:24) she kept saying. I told her that we did spank but certainly not in public. She wasn't following what I was saying, so she asked me what I meant. I said that in Nebraska, you can't spank your children in public for fear that someone would turn you into Social Services for child abuse and you could get your child taken away from you. I could tell she was having a difficult time believing me. She laughed and said that wasn't the case in the South. She said you could go to Walmart, and if your kid was misbehaving, you could take a belt off the rack, whip it, then put it right back on the rack or even ask someone if you could borrow their belt to whip your child with. She said if you didn't do something about your child misbehaving, people would actually give you a dirty look wondering why you weren't whipping them. Compliant behavior was an expectation in the South, and if not, there would be consequences. It was called Corporal Punishment. I looked it up.

According to Google, "Corporal Punishment is a discipline method in which a supervising adult deliberately inflicts pain upon a child in response to a child's unacceptable behavior and/or inappropriate language. The immediate aims of such punishment are usually to halt the offense, prevent its recurrence, and set an example for others." I was as blown away by this as she was with the fact that we couldn't spank in public in Nebraska. I had never known this was legal. I asked her to elaborate more. She told me that they had something called School Corporal Punishment where in schools, if the teachers or an Administrator were given permission from parents, they could physically punish a child for misbehaving. We talked for hours about this. I was intrigued and couldn't hear enough. I then explained to Quiniyah that Nelsyn had been through a lot with the other baby's adoption that didn't go through, and he was probably acting out for a number of reasons: one being that he didn't know for sure if we were going to be able to keep this baby, two that he was exhausted from the trip, and three, he missed seeing me and it was probably hard for him that I was not giving him my full attention. She understood…I think.

After we were done talking about Corporal Punishment, the conversation started to get personal. Quiniyah opened up to me about the reason she was placing her baby for adoption. With tear-filled eyes, she looked at me and told me the most unimaginable…she had been raped. To make the unthinkable worse, she found herself pregnant. Quiniyah said there was no other option in her mind but to have an abortion. She couldn't imagine having a child where every time she looked at her, she was reminded of her rapist.

Plus, she said she could never run the risk of keeping the baby because if her assailant ever found out about the baby, he would have parental rights. I was like, "What?" Again I was blown away. I had no idea, but it's true that in the United States, it varies by state on which one affords the rapist parental rights or not. I could hardly believe what I had just heard. All of it was unreal to me. I told her I was sorry that she had to go through all that, that I couldn't even begin to imagine what she was feeling. Quinyah then said she had every intention of aborting the baby even went as far as looking up abortion clinics in the phone book. She said she called the first number in the Yellow Pages under the title, Abortion. The person who answered had the gentlest voice ever and listened intently to what Quiniyah had been through, then the woman on the phone told her that she wasn't going to talk her out of abortion, but she wanted her to know that there were other options, such as keeping her baby or placing her child for adoption. Even after talking to this nice woman, Quiniyah still planned on aborting her baby. She didn't have the money for an abortion, but somehow had secured it. Quiniyah made an appointment and went to the abortion clinic. She said she was second in line to go back to the procedure room, where they performed the abortions when she heard that nice woman's voice in her head telling her she had other options. Quiniyah immediately got up, left the clinic, and didn't look back.

I am convinced this had to be a miracle from God because, as she told me before, once she said she would do something, she kept her word. So for her to back out of a planned abortion, it had to be God. Even though she knew she wouldn't be able to keep the baby, she had made the decision then and there that she would never abort this child growing in her womb.

You could have heard a pin drop in the room. I had tears in my eyes, and I held on to Paelyn extra tight, knowing that she had been that close to being aborted. She was truly a miracle baby, and her mom was one of the bravest women I knew.

Quiniyah said she had to figure out a way to carry the baby to term yet adopt her out without anyone knowing about her origin. She said that if her boyfriend (who was the father to her son) knew she had been raped and was pregnant with someone else's child, he would have left her. If her family knew she was pregnant, they would make her keep the baby. She was in a no-win situation.

Quiniyah came up with a well-thought-out plan. Since she was a bit of a larger woman, although she could not physically hide a pregnancy forever, no one would ever guess she was already pregnant. Time was definitely on her side. Quiniyah would have intercourse with her boyfriend. A couple of weeks later, she'd announce her "pregnancy." No one would think twice about her being pregnant, there would be no second thought about who the father was. She did her research and placed a call to the New Beginnings adoption agency and made the necessary arrangements for adoption.

Next, she would carry her child to term with everyone in her family thinking she was just six months pregnant. Then, once she went into actual labor, she would leave her home without anyone knowing where she went, go to a hospital three hours away, have the baby, and then place her for adoption. Lastly, she would come home from the hospital without her child, telling everyone that she had died since she was three months premature.

Quiniyah said she was right on track with her plan. Everything she had just told me was hard to imagine someone going through. I was truly amazed at her courage and unselfish plan to not only save Paelyn's life but give her a better life with a mother and a father who would love her and be able to provide for her.

We stayed up all night talking. I finally fell asleep around 4 am with Paelyn lying right beside me. That was short-lived because when the nurse came in to check on Quiniyah, she saw us sleeping together and said that the baby couldn't sleep with me, that she had to sleep in her bassinet, with her birth mother, or go back to the nursery. I was so tired I didn't feel like even arguing with her. We let the nurse take Paelyn back to the nursery for the remainder of the night. Quiniyah and I slept hard for about 4 hours.

Sunday morning at 6:00 am signaled the seventy-two-hour mark of when Quiniyah could sign relinquishments for her child. Never before was I so confident in something as I was in her signing. As soon as we woke up Sunday, Quiniyah called Olevia and told her she was ready to do it. Inside my mind, I was praising God for His goodness and faithfulness.

We were both exhausted from staying up all night talking, yet we had a baby to take care of. The nurse wheeled her bassinet into the hospital room. I wanted to change her into her Hello Kitty going-home outfit that Nana gave her, but decided to wait until it was actually time to leave. Even though the 72 hours were up, there was always that chance Quiniyah could still change her mind. Shortly after, Olevia arrived with the relinquishment paperwork for her to sign. I was so happy once she signed those papers, yet still burdened with the emotions of the past three days, actually more like the past 16 years since we first began our journey to becoming parents.

I was so suddenly overcome with emotion that I excused myself from the hospital room. I went to the nearest family bathroom and locked myself in the room. I took out my cell phone and dialed my parents' number. They answered. I reassured them that everything was fine; in fact, it was great, then I physically broke down and began sobbing. It was the loudest, most ugly cry I've ever cried before in my life, a wail littered with exhaustion and relief. A sob where no words were needed. Just someone to listen to. I know my parents felt helpless, being so far away, but I just needed them so badly to listen. It was like a dam had broken, and water was gushing out of control, with violent waves of emotions hitting the banks. It was a build-up of anguish, stress, raging hormones, years of waiting for a child, years of trying for children, everything that had to have been brewing for the past 16 years, that had finally come to a head and came crashing out of my body through my flood of tears. It was a major release for me. I sobbed for a good couple of minutes before finally regaining my composure. Just like that, I stopped crying. A huge load had just been lifted from my mind, body, and spirit. I remember feeling so much better. I thanked them for being there for me and promised I would call them soon.

I went back to the hospital room, and Quiniyah said, "You've been crying, haven't you?" I said, "Yes, and so have you." We hugged each other tight. Our family was finally complete, and we were almost at the finish line. I could finally see the light at the end of the tunnel we had traveled through for many years, and it was shining brightly.

There was a knock at the door; it was the nurse. She was there to remove Quiniyah's stitches from her c-section she had had just three days prior and examine her to make sure she was fit to be discharged from the hospital. I asked if I could somehow help, and Quiniyah asked me if I could help hold her tummy up so the nurse could take out the stitches more easily. So I did. I was amazed at how just what seemed like moments earlier, we were complete strangers and then here I was so close to her during a very private moment. It was an honor to help her and be there with her. The nurse removed the stitches in silence and finished her examination of Quiniyah. She was officially discharged and could leave when she was ready.

After the nurse left, Quiniyah told me she needed her privacy. She said she was going to call her mother. I couldn't take Paelyn out of the room as she wasn't yet officially discharged by her doctor, yet there was no way she could stay in the room as she could start crying and her mom might hear it and wonder about it. Then there was the need for privacy. What was I going to do? I thought of a plan. I told Quiniyah I was going to take Paelyn with me into the bathroom to give her some privacy. I stayed there while she was on the phone. We were in that bathroom for almost an hour while Quiniyah talked to her mom. I ran the water in the sink to provide an extra element of privacy, hoping it'd drown out the sound so I couldn't hear what she was saying to her mother. Paelyn and I sat in the bathtub of that bathroom for that hour, her sleeping in my arms the entire time. The only thing I could hear was when Quiniyah first got on the phone telling her mom, "It's over, she died, my baby is gone" followed by intense sobbing. It took everything out of me not to go to her side and console her, but I knew I had to keep Paelyn quiet otherwise, her cry would have blown her cover.

When Quiniyah was done, she got out of her bed and opened the door. It was over. I hugged her close and whispered to her how proud I was of her for what she had just done. Quinyah said she had never before lied to her mom and she hated that she had told her such a huge lie, but it was necessary to let Paelyn go and be with her new family.

I let Shawn know Quiniyah's examination was over and he could come back into the hospital room. Shortly after, the baby's doctor came in and performed a thorough examination of Paelyn. The doctor said everything checked out and then he signed her discharge papers. We were all free to leave.

We gathered our things. We took off Paelyn's hospital clothes and changed her into her Hello Kitty gown and hat. Gently, we placed her into her car seat. Olevia was there, and she and Quiniyah had already made plans for her to go to a nearby hotel. She could stay at the hotel as long as she needed to or until she was physically and emotionally ready to travel back to her home. We hugged long and hard and said our goodbyes. We exchanged phone numbers. I knew in my heart that even though we had grown so close, we wouldn't probably ever hear from her again. We respected her decision to have a closed adoption, but it made it extra hard to say goodbye since we had grown so close. How could she ever know how much she meant to us?

It was time for all of us to leave. We went one way and Olevia and Quiniyah went the other. It broke my heart to pieces to see Quiniyah leave without her child, but at the same time, my heart was so full of love for our new daughter. I knew what a gift we had in Paelyn.

I couldn't believe it was all over. Paelyn was officially ours.

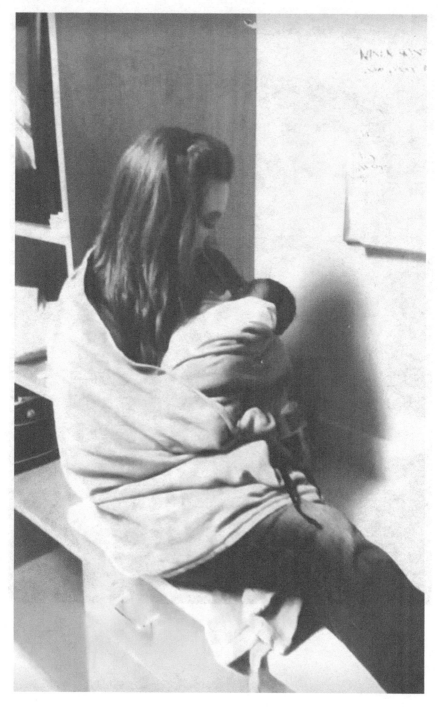

CHAPTER 5

A couple of weeks after I returned to work from my maternity leave with Paelyn, the day just so happened to be Administrative Professionals Day. As a gift, one of my bosses, Lori, gave me a book; a devotional titled "God's Whispers to a Woman's Heart" by Cindi McMenamin. In the pocket-sized devotional was one of those ribbon bookmarks that is attached to the book. I turned to the pages that the bookmark had been pre-placed between, pages 36-37. I couldn't believe what I was reading. Page 37's devotion was titled "I Don't Make Mistakes." It instantly took me back to when my dear grandma had called us when our adoption didn't go through with baby Pehrsyn and what she had said, "And honey, God doesn't make mistakes." I could feel tears burning my eyes. Even though everything had turned out beautifully with Paelyn, all those feelings of when that adoption failed with Pehrsyn came rushing back to me. I was reminded of the hurt, but also of God's faithfulness. Here is the devotion on Page 37:

I Don't Make Mistakes

"He is the Rock, his works are perfect; and all his ways are just." Deuteronomy 32:4

Admit it, My child. You've second-guessed me—on more than one occasion. As if your way of working out a situation would have been far better than Mine. Even though you sometimes can't see it, My ways are perfect. I am incapable of making a mistake. I see the beginning and the end, the temporary and the eternal. So, I never make mistakes. Will you trust Me with what looks like inconvenient timing? Will you trust Me with your world turning upside down if that is the case? Will you trust that I am in control and I wouldn't have things any other way right now? I know what I'm doing in all that I'm allowing in your life right now. And I will complete the work I have begun in you until the day of Christ Jesus (Philippians 1:6). Lord, help me to trust You every step of the way so I don't lean on my own understanding, but rest in the shadow of Your wings.

"God thunders wondrously with his voice; he does great things that we cannot fathom." Job 37:5 English Standard Version

It's always bedtime when the children ask the deep questions: where did I come from, why was I adopted, why did my birth mother have other kids but not keep me, who do I look like, do you think I got my athleticism from my birth father, will I ever get to meet my birth family, on and on. I don't have most of the answers. However, my prayer is that one day we will all become one great big family: us, birth mothers, birth siblings, birth families, maybe even birth fathers if that is God's will. Whatever is best for our children.

I wrote this book so that our children could have in writing their birth stories so they may know how much they were loved by their birth mothers and wanted by us. Hopefully, our children will gain an appreciation of what everyone all went through to get them to where they are today. I dream they will share their birth stories with their children, grandchildren, and future generations.

There may be couples out there who read this who are in similar situations. I hope they can draw hope from our story and have a family of their own someday. Whether it be experiencing infertility for years and fighting to have a baby of their own blood - to those who have drained finances and exhausted all other options and have now surrendered and are ready to experience the beautiful gift of adoption. Please don't give up on your dream to become a family!

I pray there are birth mothers out there who will not feel so alone after reading this. That they will feel appreciated and loved for the very unselfish gift of life they gave and the adoption plan they made for their children. Loved and appreciated words birth mothers may never have heard before.

Lastly, my hope is that adoptees everywhere who read this book will know they are loved completely by both their birth mothers and their adoptive families. Your birth mothers are so brave. So much love. So much sacrifice. All for you.

I thank God for allowing me to be the mother to Myles, Nelsyn, and Paelyn. I think of the lyrics from the song "Trust in God" by Elevation Worship, inspired by the verse from Psalm 34:4 "I sought the Lord and He heard and He answered." God Himself knows that we have been seeking Him for years wondering what His plan for us to be a family would be. When I finally held Myles in my arms for the first time, I knew God hadn't left us nor forsaken us. He knew exactly what we needed when we needed it.

I thank my husband, Shawn for sticking by my side in the good times and bad, for not giving up on me when I thought I just couldn't move forward anymore. I thank you for being the Christian father to our children that they need you to be. I love you and can't wait for the next 28 years together.

I thank our parents, siblings, and families who have supported us prayerfully throughout all these years. You were there for us when we needed you most. Our dreams became your dreams and you have completely accepted and loved our children from the moment you first saw them. We are all one beautiful family, and I love you all dearly.

I thank our grandmother, our dearest Nana (Myles' biological grandmother who is truly grandma to all three of our children). Your love for all of us is genuine and real and you spoil the grandkids rotten!

I thank Ms. Diane for the hospitality and love she showed our family. You will always hold a special place in our hearts and we can't wait to visit you again.

I thank An Open Door adoption agency in Georgia and New Beginnings adoption agency in Mississippi for caring for our children's birth mothers and supporting Shawn and me while we all went through the adoption process.

I thank all of our close friends, work families, and neighbors who have been there for us over the years, supporting us during our super amazing highs and terrible depressing lows.

I thank you, Myles, Nelsyn, and Paelyn, for being our children. You each bring your Dad and me so much joy and we love you deeply.

Last , but certainly not least , I thank Ariana , Kadenya , and Quiniyah. I wouldn't be the mother I am today without you. I admire your absolute fortitude to make an adoption plan for your baby. You each carried a child in your womb knowing that you wouldn't keep him. You made sure you took care of your body so that your baby could grow strong and healthy inside of you, knowing you wouldn't keep her. You planned and persevered when I'm sure you felt like giving up, giving in. Nothing could've prepared you to do what you did. Nothing could have prepared you for that first hello and that last goodbye. I saw how brave you were when you relinquished your child. You are all beautiful, brave women. Thank you. All of our love to you now and forever.

"For this child, I prayed; and the LORD has granted me the petition that I made to him." 1 Samuel 1:27

Made in the USA
Monee, IL
20 February 2025

12506727R00049